MAKING THE SYSTEM WORK FOR YOU:

THE ALEXANDER NORTON STORY

BY LORI LATRICE SYKES, PHD

MAKING THE SYSTEM WORK FOR YOU:

THE ALEXANDER NORTON STORY

BY LORI LATRICE SYKES, PHD

COPYRIGHT 2008

ISBN 978-0-6151-9355-7

To Emir Kamelle Sykes

CHAPTER 1

SOCIOECONOMIC STATUS IN AMERICA:

FROM SLAVERY TO FREEDOM

Many racial and ethnic minorities groups have worked hard to become owners in American society. Yet few have had to move from being assets to owners. Such is the case of blacks in America. In this chapter, the socioeconomic status and wealth of blacks at various points in time is examined with a particular emphasis on the role of government in limiting the ability of blacks to accumulate various forms of asset ownership. These significant points in time include Antebellum America, the 1860s to the 1940s, the post-World War II era and the post-Civil Rights era. Each provides a backdrop for understanding the Alexander Norton story.

Sociologists have an interest in understanding under what circumstances some individuals and groups come to have wealth while others do not. What measures are or have been taken by the dominant group to secure wealth and limit wealth levels and avenues of wealth accumulation for subordinate groups? One indicator of how much anything matters in American society is how that indicator is reflected by law. The law represents in many ways who and what is valued in society and who and what is socially acceptable in society. Therefore, examining the role of the legal system and the role of government in particular in limiting access to certain types of assets for different groups helps account, in part, for variations in the levels and types of assets owned both historically and currently. Efforts to limit socioeconomic status and restrict various types of asset ownership for blacks relative to whites at various points in time illustrate of this point.

During Antebellum America the principles of black inferiority and white superiority were adapted at all levels of society, eventually becoming the bedrock of the American social structure for generations to follow. Slavery was a difficult time, to say the least, for all blacks. Blacks were income and asset poor. The first blacks to reach America's shores were probably not slaves and likely came to the United States as servants during the early 1600s as did many whites during that time. However, during the 1640s, there was a dramatic shift in the status of blacks. While white servants could look towards freedom blacks became slaves for life. This period of transformation in the status of blacks in America occurred ironically at a time when people of European heritage were arguing for democracy and seeking freedom and equality for themselves. These same freedom fighters established a racialized social system in the Americas that insisted upon the importance of racial differences as a justification of economic inequality. Africans would eventually be viewed as natural slaves while Europeans would be perceived as potential citizens.

Between the 1640s and early 1700s, Africans in America went from being servants or free persons to having their children regarded as slaves, being treated as property and eventually being denied the right to vote or the right to testify in court. America during this time became increasingly dependent upon black slave labor, benefitting from this less expensive form of labor in many tangible and subtle ways. Owning a black slave was one pathway to asset accumulation. Plantation owners, corporations and nations received great economic advantages during this period.

Ownership of black slaves gave settlers greater prestige. Many political leaders owned slaves and the number of slaves owned was a barometer of their wealth, status and power. Many importers of slaves became eligible for land grants. In South Carolina, for example, every free person over the age of 16 received 150 acres for each male slave or male servant imported and 100 acres for every female slave or female servant imported under sixteen years of age. At the end of a servant's term, the servant received 40 acres. For blacks, who were overwhelmingly slaves and not servants their term of service, was not expected to end so they received nothing. Unlike the case for slaves, the economic and social inferiority of servants was temporary.

The United States Congress officially abolished the slave trade in the early 1800s, which signaled a transformation in the status of blacks. The abolition of the slave trade did not mean that the enslavement system had ended, instead it entered a new phase. The American plantation system became increasing dependent upon natural increase to reproduce slave labor. Consequently, control over the fertility and the reproductive freedom of blacks was critical. Based on data collected from the first US Census we know that the black population numbered 757,000 or 19% of the total population. Between 1790 and 1880, the black population grew rapidly at a rate of over 2% per year to 4.4 million.

Slave owners had an economic incentive to control black fertility. The fact that the offspring of slaves became the property of the slave owners

> made control of reproduction a central aspect of white's subjugation of African people in America. It marked blacks from the beginning as objects who decisions about

> reproduction should be subject to social regulation rather
> than to their own will, (Roberts 1997, p. 23).

Not only was the fertility of enslaved blacks controlled, but so was the socioeconomic status of both enslaved and free blacks, as was every other aspect of black life.

In Delaware, it was illegal for more than 12 free blacks to hold a meeting past 10 pm in the winter without at least three respectable whites present. During this period, the occupational choices for all blacks were restricted, educational opportunities were limited and wages were below what blacks deserved. Blacks were over represented in service occupations.

A review of the current literature on blacks and business ownership might lead to the conclusion that blacks have no legitimate history of entrepreneurship with the exception of a few well known black business owners. However, some scholars have shown that many Africans brought with them entrepreneurial skills and values and adapted them in a way that enabled the individuals, the businesses and the community to survive under oppressive conditions. As a result, many blacks ran businesses and shared information about entrepreneurship informally because learning and making money were hazardous to their health, particularly during this period in American history.

Black businesses during the antebellum era in the U.S. were largely located in the Northeast and provided services to other blacks. There was a high correlation at this time between the size of the black population in a given area and to the number of black owned businesses. Catering was among one of the more profitable industries for blacks as were hairdressing, tailoring, cleaning and dyeing, barbering, shoemaking and blacksmithing. Whites did a lot, often times with support from the government, to keep blacks from competing openly and freely in the open market. The most obvious case is slavery. Despite the history and legacy of slavery, blacks were still able to demonstrate their business savvy. This was evidenced by their ability to save and purchase the freedom of family members and through the decision-making authority bestowed upon them by their owners. This decision-making authority often led to the development of independent business relations between slaves and others. Butler recounts many empirical examples of blacks and their participation in economic activity, from the works of Richard Allen and entrepreneurs in the segregated south through the present. He notes that the defining character of the black experience when compared with that of whites was the outright racism and discrimination that kept blacks from competing freely in the market place.

Ironically as blacks were prohibited and restricted by law from freely participating in economic activity, their communities became an avenue of social mobility for other non-white groups in America. One need only look to middleman minorities like the Jews in New York City or a more contemporary example, Koreans in Los Angeles.

The free black experience was by no means homogeneous. Farm owners of both genders had significantly more wealth than unskilled laborers. Black women, according to the study, who worked as domestic servants, washerwomen, and seamstresses accumulated more property than laborers. Black women working in service organizations such as nurses, midwives and boarding house operators, also accumulated significantly more than unskilled women.

Among female-headed households the complexion gap takes on a different form than it does among male-headed households. At the conditional mean of wealth distribution the complexion gap virtually disappears for black males but remains at about 20 percent among women. However, the study goes on to show that despite mulatto women's ability to accumulate more personal wealth than other black women, mulatto women did not accumulate as much wealth as either mulatto men or other black men counterparts. The complexion gap, according to the author, reinforced a gender gap, which left black women householders at the lowest level of the economic ladder.

After the Civil War, the socioeconomic status of blacks remained significantly below that of whites. Hostility towards blacks increased after the Civil War. This hostility towards blacks manifested itself in a series of political actions that restricted economic opportunities for blacks in the areas of education, occupation, income and home ownership.

These challenges included inequalities in expenditures for black and White schools. Between 1875 and 1890 for example, $1.10 to $1.20 was spent on the teacher's salaries of white children compared to only $1.00 for the teacher's salaries of black children. By the first decade of the twentieth century, the ratio of black-white per capita expenditures exceeded six-to-one. Not only were black teachers paid less but black schools particularly those in the South, received smaller proportions of the funds for transportation for schools and black schools had higher pupil-teacher ratios and smaller proportions of expenditures for buildings and equipment relative to whites. Racial disparities in educational expenditures continued until about the 1940s where until that time blacks received anywhere from one-third to two-fifths of the amount spent for each white child. Stanley Liberson, author of <u>A Piece of the Pie</u>, cites the educational needs of whites and a lack of sympathy on the part of whites for quality black education as two key factors affecting black education. It is also important to note that schools in the South lagged behind schools in the North and that blacks in the South lagged behind whites in the South. So not only were blacks more disadvantaged than whites in the South but they were also disadvantaged relative to whites in the North as well as blacks in the North.

Education is a significant indicator of socioeconomic status because it becomes an important avenue of mobility for all groups. The relationship between assimilation, place and race and gender differentials in education is important here as well. Educational institutions in the North served as a means of assimilation for immigrants. It was in the educational institutions that immigrants would learn to become Americans. For blacks, who prior to the Great Migration were overwhelming living in the south, resistance to educating them was strong and persistent and was evidenced in the educational system in the North as well. Schools were not a mechanism by which blacks would be assimilated into mainstream American society. Instead, schools were the training grounds where blacks would learn their appropriate place in the social structure----at the very bottom.

Race and gender differences in educational attainment for blacks relative to whites revealed patterns similar to those found in occupational and income. At the beginning of the 20th century, more black males for example worked as servants or waiters than as other workers. The higher the black population in a particular city the higher the percentage of servants that was black. Where blacks made up less than 10 percent of a given city's population, blacks made up at least half of all servants. Few, if any, blacks worked outside that field for some time. Occupational opportunities would not open up for black males or black females until the number of whites was small enough that they could concentrate on even more desirable positions. Occupational opportunities would then be open to blacks.

In the early 1900s, discrimination was evident in education, occupation and earnings and also in land and home ownership. An Associated Press (AP) investigation found evidence of over one hundred land takings in 13 southern and border states. In these cases alone 406 black landowners lost over 24,000 acres of farmland and timberland in addition to 85 smaller properties such as stores and city lots. Almost all of the property identified in the investigation is owned by whites or corporations and is valued in the tens of millions of dollars.

The investigation also uncovered that in 1910, blacks owned at least 15 million acres of farmland. Today, blacks own just over 1 million acres of farmland and are part owners of another 1.07 million acres. It should be noted that the number of white farmers has also declined over time, however black ownership has declined 2.5 times faster than white ownership. Surely, migration from the south to the north accounts for some of the decline in black land ownership but land takings also contribute to the decline.

The extent to which land takings have impacted wealth in the black community may never be known. The AP found that there are several gaps in public records and that existing records have been altered. Moreover, it is noted that about a third of the county courthouses in Southern and border states have burned since the Civil War. Discrimination against blacks continued in the early 1900s, at the same time that opportunities for increasing the socioeconomic status of blacks were widening. Large numbers of black men and women were migrating to the North. Nearly half a million blacks left the South between the end of the Civil War and 1920 and another 750,000 joined them by the end of the 1920s. The migration of Southern Blacks to Northern cities was a time of great demographic change that affected the population size and composition of these cities in profound ways. In just two decades the black population in New York more than tripled.

Blacks were attracted to the North because of employment opportunities there. Prospects for earning a living wage were much better in the North at this time than in the South. Another important factor was that there was a labor shortage in the North as a direct consequence of the beginnings of World War I, which led to restrictions on immigration. Prior to that time, blacks were relegated to low paying and unskilled occupations such as laborers, janitors and porters. "The industrial semi-skilled and skilled positions that gave millions of immigrants the chance to climb out of poverty were off-limits."

Despite gains made during the World War I era, there were still racial gaps in income, educational attainment, occupational choice, and business ownership. Whites did not face the same type of discrimination in business ownership. There are few accounts that mirror that of the destruction of Tulsa, Oklahoma, or that of the booming economic activity in Durham. Tulsa has been described by some as the site of the worst race riots in American history. In 1921, the city was engaged in a battle that cost scores of blacks their lives and countless others, their wealth and livelihood. According to the findings of the Oklahoma Commission to Study the Tulsa Race Riot of 1921 (2001), 35-square-blocks of the black community were destroyed on May 31, 1921. A young shoe shining male was accused of raping a white woman in the middle of the day in a public elevator. He was arrested and angry whites, looking to take the law into their own hands were intent upon lynching him. However, a group of armed blacks attempted to protect him. A fight broke out between the two groups, a shot rang out and the rest as they say is history. Shortly thereafter, the black community was ablaze.

The commission's report demonstrates that blacks tried to protect their community but their efforts were no match for the bombs that were dropped from airplanes from above. The report recalls how blacks were sent to camps. In the prologue to the report, State Representative Don Ross provides a historical context for understanding how the black community in Tulsa became not only established but also how it came to be known as "Black Wall Street" because of the concentration of black wealth that existed here. The Honorable Don Ross takes us back to the Revolutionary War and notes that the constitution sanctioned slavery. He adds that broken treaties and efforts to exterminate Native Americans led to the migration of this population towards the Ohio Valley and other treaties led to Native American settling in the south. He notes that southern tribes had slaves, however they also offered refuge to runaway slaves and in some cases gave them tribal membership and rights.

Ross adds, as part of the Tulsa Race Riot of 1921 report, that the removal of tribes from their land and cruelty of the "Trail of Tears" linked blacks and Native Americans in an important way. He notes that many former slaves were registered as members of the tribes and offered a sanctuary in the land allotments. He further adds that after Oklahoma was opened up for settlement, more and more blacks from the south saw Oklahoma as the "promised land." He further notes that there were at least 50 all-black towns, several of which were very prosperous like Boley and Langston.

The report provides a window into the level of asset ownership that existed in Tulsa before the race riots. For example it is noted that in 1908, O.W. Gurley constructed the first building which was a rooming house. Gurley also purchased 30 or 40 acres, plotted them and would sell them to blacks only. J.B. Stradford represents another example. Stradford built a hotel valued at the time at $75,000.

Blacks lost everything in Tulsa as a result of the riots and the aftermath. Officially the direct economic cost was estimated at $1.5 million but records indicate that blacks filed claims of about $4 million. For example, Dr. Motley claimed his surgical equipment and medicines as well as book cases, a set of Harvard classics, a library table, a Steinway piano, Rodgers silverware and other items. Still others filed claims for livestock, rental property and other materials. However, every single claim brought by blacks was denied. The only person to be compensated, white or black was a white shop owner. The shop owner was compensated for guns taken from his shop during the riot.

The black community of Tulsa was home about 11,000 with almost 200 businesses. Specifically, there were 5 doctors, a chiropractor, 2 dentists and 3 lawyers. There were also two newspapers, a library, 2 schools, a hospital and a public health service office. Likewise, there were also fraternal lodges and churches.

The commission looked not only at the historical context in which Black Wall Street developed or the property loss, but it also assessed state and city accountability and argued that responsibility for the Tulsa riot "represented the breakdown of the rule of law." The breakdown of law was at the heart of the riot, scholars have argued. Tulsa failed to take action to protect the black community against the riot and that city officials deputized men after the riot broke out. Many of these deputies participated in the burning of the black community. There is clear and convincing evidence to support the contention that the riot was as bad as it was because of the actions of Tulsa officials.

It is also noted that the National Guard which was called in to help with the riot behaved favorably on the onset, restoring order in some instances and some would argue protected the lives of blacks in the community. However, it is also noted that the Guard may have acted unconstitutionally. The guards, it is noted, arrested every black resident they could find in Tulsa and then took them into custody which left the black community unprotected and vulnerable. In short, the Guard helped to disarm black residents, which left their property defenseless. Likewise, it is noted that after the riots efforts to rebuild the black community were blocked. This was accomplished by making the cost of rebuilding the community extremely expensive. A zoning ordinance that required the use of fireproof material in rebuilding making rebuilding in the black community "prohibitively expensive" was passed following the riots.

Blacks faced barriers in their professional occupational pursuits as well as barriers in their efforts to secure and maintain wealth. In Chicago for example between 1920 and 1940, the percentage of black males in professional occupations increased from 9%-16% but was still well below the percentage of white males who were white-collar workers and the numbers doing skilled manual work had not risen at all. For black women very little had changed during that same twenty-year period. In 1920, over 60% of black women worked as domestic servants in Chicago and by 1940 that figure had not changed.

Blacks were disadvantaged not only because of the inferior education available to them in the South or because they were unfamiliar with the urban labor market. In addition, there was a dual labor market at play. This dual market was defined by primary jobs and secondary jobs requiring varying levels of education and employment experience and was divided on the basis of race. So, there were black jobs and white jobs. Even though opportunities were greater than they were in the South they were still relatively low compared to opportunities available to whites, both the native-born and the foreign-born. The exclusion of blacks in many labor unions did not help either and was a reflection of hostility towards blacks in general and towards black workers in particular.

Blacks continued to migrate to the North until the Great Depression when economic opportunities were limited. Although everyone living in the U.S. in the early 1930s was affected by the Great Depression, some argue that blacks were more adversely affected than were most whites. Prior to the Great Depression, blacks were already poor relative to whites and many remained so during the economic boom surrounding the First World War U.S. policies aimed at assisting Americans during this economic crisis improved the status of whites and worsened the situation for blacks. For example, farm owners were given economic incentives to remove land in an effort to limit supplies and increase prices. One consequence of this program was a reduction in the amount of farmland, and fewer tenants and fewer laborers who were black. Coalitions of Southern politicians made sure that planters would not be eligible for pensions and unemployment insurance. For all intents and purposes, the deal was not new. Blacks were left out of this new safety net system as they had been left out of other opportunities for social and economic mobility.

The period between the 1940s and the 1970s was a time of dramatic social and demographic change for most Americans including blacks. Technological advances in agriculture and a reduction in farm production had a particularly strong effect on blacks. Fewer jobs and lower wages were just two implications as blacks moved off farms and out of white kitchens. For blacks who owned farms, they were often displaced for lack of capital required in the new age of farming. Between 1940-1960, the number of blacks living on farms in the South declined dramatically.

Occupational prestige improved for some black men and black women as did incomes for millions of black men and black women that left the south for the north between the 1940s and the 1960s. In 1960, the incomes of black women were double the income levels in the 1940s. It should be noted that whites also did quite well during this twenty-year period. The gains that blacks made did not lead to race-parity.

While the incomes of black women increased between 1940 and 1960, white women still made more than Black women. This was true despite the fact that black women have a longer history of labor force participation relative to other racial and ethnic sub-groups of women. She shows that when black females born between 1946-1955, were coming of age, black women had more experience in the labor force than white women. This was due in large part to economic necessity and the devaluation of black women relative to white women. Black women, due to their experience with both racism and sexism during this period, had earnings behind those of black men, white men and white females. Black women also delayed marriage, bore fewer children and increased their levels of education and occupational prestige as did many white women.

Since black women's labor force participation was already significantly higher than white women's, the positive effects experienced by white women as a result of delays in marriage, declines in fertility and increases on various socioeconomic indicators were not felt among black women.

For the early baby boom cohort, black women's earnings were greater than white women's average earnings, while black men's earnings were 85% of the earnings of white men with comparable levels of education. Gender equality, however was not achieved by either whites or blacks, but black women's hourly earnings were much closer to those of black men than white women's earnings were to white men's.

The social benchmarks achieved by blacks during the post-1960s era were due in part to the Civil Rights Movement. Since the enslavement era, blacks in America have struggled against social norms, laws and ordinances that restricted virtually every aspect of their lives. Between the end of the Civil War in 1865 and the civil rights movement, deliberate efforts were made to limit black mobility, both spatially and socially, in such areas as education, occupation, and housing. Redlining, restrictive covenants, discriminatory lending practices, intimidation and physical violence were among the strategies targeted towards blacks. This period of over one hundred years was filled with protest and promise.

The period between 1946-1954 may be characterized as an era of rising expectations culminating in Brown v. Board of Education, (1954), which found the separate but equal principle to be unconstitutional. The civil rights movement, which began in Montgomery, Alabama in 1955, was the first major challenge to a national postwar consensus of rising expectations about race in America.

Omi and Winant authors of <u>Racial Formation,</u> characterized the decade that followed as a period of tremendous conflict in which the meaning of race was politically contested and where race occupied a position in American politics that had not been seen since the Civil War era a century earlier. Thus the events of the 1960s, collectively known as the civil rights movement, were viewed as a period of rebellion by blacks seeking mainstream inclusion and equal access to social institutions. The civil rights movement was a network of activists who worked to force the government to pass and implement laws guaranteeing equal opportunity for racial and ethnic minorities and women. The Civil Rights Act of 1964 banned racial discrimination in employment. The Voting Rights Act of 1965 forced the political enfranchisement of blacks by eliminating literacy tests and other discriminatory tactics. The Fair Housing Act of 1968 banned discrimination in the rental and sale of housing units.

Morris who has written about the civil rights movement argued that the impact of the civil rights movement was twofold. First, the civil rights movement altered a system that severely restricted the personal freedom of blacks and disfranchised them in the formal political sense. Second, the civil rights movement provided other oppressed groups with organizational tactical models, allowing them to enter directly into the political arena.

This period filled with hope and symbolic promise did not last long. The disappearance of work from urban areas in the Northeast and the Midwest is often cited as the root of contemporary racial differences between blacks and whites. In addition to the exodus of manufacturing and union jobs in these regions, the concentration of black populations is also cited as an important determinant of racial differences in socioeconomic status between blacks and whites. Whites, it is argued, became more discriminatory as they perceived a threat of increased economic competition from a growing number of non-whites, in this case blacks.

A review of how blacks have endeavored to move from being assets to being owners was conducted. Specifically, the socioeconomic status and asset accumulation during significant periods in American history were noted. The chapter focused on black asset ownership in Antebellum America, in the 1860s-1940s, in the post-World War II era and the post-Civil Rights era.

This review shows how blacks have endeavored to move from assets to owners and how these efforts have been met by the dominant group with a range of responses from reluctant hospitality to violent, often times government sanctioned, hostility. Despite the absolute gains made by the black population, the advances pale in comparison to the gains made relative to the dominant group, whites. Blacks continue to lag behind whites on various social indicators especially where asset ownership is concerned. Even in the midst of the growing gap between blacks and whites, blacks have not only desired wealth but obtained it in spite of adversity. The story of Alexander Norton is truly illustrative of that fact.

CHAPTER 2

COMING OF AGE IN RIDGELAND

Alexander Norton, Sr., of New Berlin, New York went from being a dishwasher to running a million dollar construction business with only a fifth-grade education, gift for math, and a dream he wanted to make a reality. How did he do it? How did he go from a life of economic insecurity to one characterized as economically empowered? More importantly, how can others make the transformation and why is such a transformation necessary in the first place? The struggle for equality, for economic empowerment for Norton and for others, especially racial and ethnic minorities, has been hard fought and at times likened to an uphill battle.

Research by scholars like Melvin Oliver and Thomas Shapiro, authors of Black Wealth White Wealth, highlighted the existence and persistence of wealth inequality in America. Economic inequality is very much alive and nowhere is that fact more evident than in the gap between whites and nonwhites on the types and levels of assets owned. Prior to Oliver and Shapiro's seminal work, economic inequality between the racial and ethnic minority groups and the racial majority group in America, was measured largely by income with little regard for assets. Given that the dialogue about racial and ethnic economic inequality centered on income, policymakers and advocacy groups worked and continue to work towards shoring up the economic security of historically disadvantaged groups.

While important, the emphasis on economic security was not and is not sufficient to address the persistent structural inequality that exists. Inequality is evidenced by continued differentiated access to the social structure for racial and ethnic minority group. The dialogue must shift from one based almost exclusively on economic security matters to one based upon economic empowerment. We are seeing somewhat of a shift in focus as several well respected, largely civil rights organizations, have made economic empowerment a centerpiece of efforts to improve the plight of racial and ethnic minorities, but what is meant by the term economic empowerment and in what ways is this term distinguishable from economic security? Alexander Norton understood this difference and longed for economic empowerment.

Economic security and economic empowerment are distinct, but related terms. Levitan (1985) writing about the American welfare system describes economic security as one's ability to meet their basic needs. The welfare system, it was argued, evolved out of a desire to provide greater economic security for all income groups; to cushion the impact of economic misfortune. It is an idea that numerous administrators have invested in, which despite historic controversies and the ultimate end to the system, as we know it, have benefited the poor and the non-poor alike.

Others define economic security by access to health, education, dwelling, information, and social protection, as well as, work-related security. In short, definitions of economic security have implicitly and explicitly focused on expanding the wage-earning capacity of Americans, including but not limited to, racial and ethnic minorities such that these individuals could meet their basic needs. Economic empowerment is much more than that. Economic empowerment is about long-term self-sufficiency; it's about economic autonomy; it's about upsetting the social structure and resisting the status quo. It's about more than just living for the here and now, rather it's about building families, communities, and empowering groups for generations to come. Alexander Norton is a firm believer that more people can move from economic insecurity to economic empowerment and that it doesn't take a million dollar trust fund to do.

We know that like many other sociological outcomes that asset inequality is multilevel and multidimensional. At the micro-level it involves individuals, small groups and their face-to-face interactions while, the macro-level involves large groups, large-scale institutions, and/or the society at-large. Taken together the two levels provide a more complete understanding as to how society operates and under what conditions social change takes place. To date, many approaches to understanding economic inequality between racial and ethnic groups have focused on either the macro-level or the micro-level and have attributed the observed economic differences to either the shortcomings of individuals or the shortfalls of institutions. Regardless, one can think of three levels of stratification: economic empowerment, economic security, and economic insecurity. The levels take into consideration the importance of income as well as assets.

Individuals and groups that are economically insecure lack a safety net to protect them in the time of an economic storm. Individuals and groups may find themselves in this situation due to forces beyond their control or because of poor financial decisions. These individuals and groups include low-wage workers, over represented in the secondary labor market as well as the unemployed and the underemployed. Even individuals and groups that are over represented in the informal or underground economy may be found among the economically insecure since by definition their wages are not taxed and/or the activities for which they are engaged in place them at high risk for economic uncertainty. This type of economic uncertainty is quite different than the economic uncertainty associated with other types of economic activity such as involvement in the stock market, which will be addressed later. Alexander Norton found himself among this group especially during his early years.

There are of course varying degrees of economic insecurity, as there are varying degrees of economic security. Some individuals and groups may be more economically secure than others given variations in income levels and variations in the levels and types of assets owned. One could argue that income rich individuals who lack assets are just steps away from being among the economically insecure. As the number and levels of income and assets grows, but especially assets, the more economically secure individuals and groups become. Individuals and groups with wages, in addition to savings, are more secure than individuals and groups with wages alone. At the same time, this group may be less secure than those who have stock ownership too.

An individual who has some savings may be in a better position to handle an economic crisis, like the loss of a job, than someone without savings. However, the individual who possesses the stocks may liquefy those assets if necessary albeit with penalties, and fare better during the crisis than counterparts with fewer assets. In essence it could be argued that one's level of economic security increases as the levels and types of assets owned increases. Once an individual or group has not only wages but also access to homeownership, business ownership, savings, stock ownership, and other real estate, they have moved beyond mere economic security towards economic empowerment. Few individuals and even fewer groups reach economic empowerment

26

although it is the goal of many; it is after all the embodiment of the American Dream. Bucking the trend, Alexander Norton would eventually join the ranks of the economically empowered, unfortunately he would not find the level of racial and ethnic diversity in that category that many have dreamed would occur almost four decades after Martin Luther King, Jr.'s famous speech.

Certain groups have become economically empowered while others remain economically insecure, generation after generation. At the bases of this hierarchy, one could find a myriad of racial and ethnic groups include poor whites. Certain groups are over represented among these varying levels. It is however important to note that individuals from a number of racial and ethnic groups can be found at each level. Among the economically insecure we find the poor regardless of their race or ethnicity. We also find among this group, working-, middle-, and upper-class, Asians, Blacks, Hispanics, and Native Americans placed here by virtue of the absence of any asset holdings. Given that individuals and groups that have wages only are often a paycheck or two away from being economically insecure they are included here also.

Individuals and groups who have income and some asset holdings are relatively secure economically and can include working-, middle- and upper-class Asian, Blacks, Hispanics, Native Americans and Whites. The economically empowered consists of individuals and groups that are income rich with diverse asset holdings. Individuals with membership in the dominant racial group are more likely to be found here than are other groups. It is this group that has more power and more control over their lives than members of minority groups. They have greater life chances and exert their will over others in virtually every area of society.

While whites dominate the economically empowered category and have historically, racial and ethnic minority groups have endeavored to break through this glass ceiling in an effort to control their own destinies; to be viewed as stakeholders in the American experiment; to bequeath cultural as well as monetary capital to future generations. Yet various racial and ethnic groups in America have historically encountered barriers in trying to attain these goals although progress has been made.

There are many examples historic as well as contemporary examples of individuals who belong to various racial and ethnic minority groups who worked diligently to move not just themselves but also their group as a whole from economic insecurity to economic empowerment. Before going into great depth about the life and legacy of Alexander Norton, we will briefly review the lives of two of Norton's predecessors who also made the shift from a life of economic insecurity to one that was economically empowered. There are similarities and differences between these individuals and Alexander Norton.

Lawrence Otis Graham writes about a man who is not known to many Americans, although he may have established what Graham calls, America's first black dynasty. Senator Blanche Kelso Bruce was the first black person to ever serve a full-term from Mississippi in the United States Senate, beginning in 1875. He began life as a slave. Slaves as we know were not viewed as human beings rather as chattel or property. By definition, Bruce began his life not with wages or with assets, but as an asset of someone else. Despite Bruce's beginning as a member of a group whose members found themselves relegated to economic insecurity, he went on to become very influential and quite wealthy. Not only did he end up serving in the U.S. Senate, but he also was nominated for vice president, served as the leader of the Mississippi State Republicans, and held appointments in the Treasury Department among such Presidents as Arthur, Harrison, and McKinley. He would go on to marry a woman from an upper class, black family that only enhanced his position among the freeborn black community of his time, which would have been off limits otherwise given that he was a former slave. At the time of his marriage to Josephine, it is estimated that his net worth was in excess of $150,000. In contemporary dollars, Bruce would have been worth over $2 million dollars. Bruce escaped from slavery in 1863, according to Graham, and developed important relationships with influential whites that would place him in positions he or any of his contemporaries, black or white, thought possible. Through these relationships he was able to get elected to or appointed as county sheriff, county commissioner, and tax collector, among others in Bolivar County. He developed many skills including how to buy and foreclose on properties, which allowed him to get rental property. He would later purchase an 800-acre plantation to fund his political ambitions. He would use his assets and influence to help others, although the dynasty would end with the financial failures of subsequent generations and despite all that Bruce accomplished he was never fully accepted by the dominant racial group in America who occupied the top position in the pyramid, the economically empowered.

Using a variety of sources, Graham is able to document the level of hostility faced Bruce, in particular, but faced racial and ethnic minority groups, specifically. On the very day that Bruce was to be sworn in on the floor of the U.S. Senate, the message that his presence, despite his wealth was not welcomed was abundantly clear. The senior senator from Mississippi refused to walk Bruce down the isle for his swearing in ceremony, which was customary. A lone senator from New York, to the dismay and shock of the other senators, was willing to escort Bruce. The incident showed Bruce and to others, the level of resistance that still existed between racial and ethnic groups. Clearly, Bruce has moved up the ranks from being among the economically insecure to achieving a high level of economic security, but his access and access to others with membership in the same racial group, to economic empowerment was limited.

A more contemporary example that also examines how members of racial and ethnic minority groups endeavor to move of the socioeconomic latter from economic insecurity to economic empowerment concerns the life and times of Rev. John "Jack" Johnson. Johnson with very little formal education came to amass assets that enriched the lives of his immediate family and the communities in which he lived and worked. There are a number of similarities between Johnson and Alexander Norton from their childhood in the South to their migration to the North and beyond.

Jack Johnson, the grandson of a slave, was born in August 1909 in a small town in Mississippi called Shubuta. He was one of 16 children. He had only a few years of formal education and was given the enormous responsibility of managing the family farm at the age of 16 for a period of two when his father became ill until his father was well enough to resume its operations. As the Great Depression hit America, Johnson left the tiny town, already crippled in the clutches of sharecropping, for the North in search of employment opportunities. His sojourner led him to Albany, New York. Upon arrival he found work where he could, washing walls, floors and cleaning the streets so he could make enough money to buy the basics. After three years in Albany, he married Dorothy Mary Charles and the two had seven children[1].

Johnson also worked as a carpenter's helper and would eventually secure jobs renovating and repairing houses throughout the Capital Region. He befriended one of the partners of Albert & Kirsch, Irving Kirsch, from whom he would come to purchase 14 houses. Kirsch, born the same year as Johnson, was born in New York City and migrated to Albany in the 1940s. He and Sydney Albert were business partners for more than 60 years. They operated a multimillion-dollar real estate business in the Albany area.

Kirsch was said to have supported most of the charities, foundations and religious organizations in the greater Albany area. He was also known for helping individuals in need with new clothes or shoes for children. He gave small allowances to those being released from jail and money for special equipment for the disabled. He supported faith-based institutions from many denominations including Catholic nuns, black Baptist and Pentecostal Churches, including one founded by Johnson. Kirsch is even credited with underwriting the construction of a building for the Hebrew Academy. He was a major donor for the City of Albany Beautification project where he financed a fountain and wildflower garden in downtown Academy Park. He also was a major contributor of the Park Playhouse in Albany's Washington Park. Kirsch, with his partner Sydney Albert, secured many apartment houses and rental properties in the Capital District area, and

---

[1] "Johnson's biographical information was obtained from a variety of sources including from a document distributed at his death on July 10, 2004 entitled, A Glimpse of Life."

operated as Tri-Cities Rentals ("IRVING KIRSCH. CAPITAL REGION)." *Albany Times*
Union (Albany, NY) (August 24, 1999): B6. *New York State Newspapers*).

Kirsch and his business partner were not always remembered favorably, some accounts contend that their firm "has grown from a partnership between Albert and Kirsch in the 1960s that was documented as the largest owner of slum housing in the Capital District into a business Dun & Bradstreet Corp., the financial reporting service, estimates was worth more than $121 million in 1989 which would have placed the firm among the nation's 300 most profitable owners of apartment complexes" (FROM SLUMLORD, ALBERT BECAME PHILANTHROPIST.(Business)." *Albany Times Union (Albany, NY)* (July 15, 1990): F1). Nonetheless, the homes purchased by Johnson became a refuge for many. After repairing the units, Johnson then rented them to the economically disadvantaged for very little or at no cost. He also provided employment for many males in the community who he would allow to accompany him as he repaired homes.

Johnson was not only an excellent carpenter but he was also a member of the clergy and affiliated with the Church of God in Christ (COGIC). As part of his work with the church and his desire to improve the quality of life for himself and for others, he created an organization in the 1940s for young people that provided them with mentoring and tutorial services. Johnson provided the financial backing for these and other services provided by the club and other initiatives he started. The organization was called, the Good Samaritan Club. He is also credited with establishing a host of faith-based institutions in Connecticut and in the Mid-Hudson region of New York. Using his carpenter skills he would not only assist in the establishment of the churches but he would physically assist in the conversion of storefronts and various other buildings to be used as houses of worship. Throughout this book we will see the Alexander Norton shares with Johnson an interest in using his skills, knowledge, and wealth to help others.

Johnson, like Norton, was known as a philanthropist. Johnson assisted those in financial trouble with housing, jobs, gifts and loans, many of which he was never repaid. He was considered by many in the area to be a modern day Harriet Tubman in that during the 1930s and the 1960s, he traveled back to Mississippi to help families escape the oppressive sister systems of sharecropping and Jim Crow. It is estimated that he brought no less than 100 families some 1300 miles, from Mississippi to New York, in search of a better life. The new arrivals, many with very little resources, would stay in one of the homes he now owned at no cost to them until they could find employment and make it on their own ("Students Take Trek Through Black Culture. *Albany Times Union. Albany, NY.* July 13, 1997: D1). According to an article about Johnson, he is credited with spawning "a community of lawyers, teachers, medical technicians and business owners" ("His Drive Gave Many a Future" *Albany Times Union.* Nov 8, 1998: H1).

Johnson would establish the first day care center in Albany to be operated by blacks in Albany in 1962. The center was operational for about 10 years and was financed without support from private or governmental funds. The center with support from St. Johns COGIC, which Johnson founded, provided meals, transportation and enrichment activities for the children in his care from 6:30 am until 5:00 pm. Johnson' church and his compassion continued to grow. His contributions to the Capital Region would eventually be recognized in the 1990s when a street was named in his honor, "Rev. John (Jack) Johnson Way."

In 2001, Johns Community Development Corporation (CDC) was established. The CDC established an after-school program, a community meal program, a summer camp and a homeless prevention program. The after-school program provides Supplementary Educational Services in cooperation with the New York State Department of Education for the students of the City School District of Albany who attending middle schools that are need in improvement. The community meal program combats hunger by providing free meals to those in need; many in attendance are from the local city mission. The summer camp employs youth through a city program and the elderly through the foster grandparents program. It provides children ages 5 though 12 with instruction in math, art, reading and music. The homeless prevention program is one of a kind in the city of Albany. Through support from friends of the CDC in the New York State Assembly and Senate including Neil Breslin and Ronald Canestrari, St. Johns CDC is able to provide financial assistance to employed heads of households who are at-risk of becoming homeless due to back rent owned or mortgage owned. The organization has prevented many individuals and families from becoming homeless and hungry (www.stjohnscdc.org). After Johnson's passing on July 4, 2004, at the age of 94, a scholarship was established in his name, which provides direct financial assistance to high school seniors in the Capital Region of New York State.

Johnson is another example of an individual who started with almost nothing who grew to amass a substantial amount of wealth that he was able to use to provide a sense of economic security to others. With very little education and with only 2 shirts, a jacket and 2 pair of pants, he would go on to leave a legacy of home ownership, a tradition of self-help and desire for economic empowerment that lives on today.

Alexander Norton's sojourn began in Ridgeland, South Carolina on April 15, 1938. Al as he is affectionately known, is one of 12 children born to Willie and Sara Norton. He along with his 6 brothers and 5 sisters, were raised in a house that his father built in 1927. Ridgeland, South Carolina, like many other American communities, has its roots in the American rail system. According to town officials when the railroad was being planned in the 1800s, Grahamville, a town adjacent to Ridgeland, did not want the noise, smoke, and smell associated with the railroad. Ridgeland had just begun to develop when the Civil War ravished the area. The war left most residents living in poverty. Towards the turn of the 20th century, things began looking up for Ridgeland. Capital from wealthy outsiders led to the establishment of timber companies among other enterprises. Local residents began businesses and small industries. Ridgeland, South Carolina and its residents were filled with a great deal of optimism and hope for the future that was until the Great Depression. As Ridgeland and the nation came out of the depression, the town was able to grow and attract tourists especially given its location on U.S. Highway 17.

Today, Ridgeland is home to about 2,500 residents. About 45% of residents in 2000 were white and almost 50% were black. Most of the residents reported that they were renters as opposed to homeowners. In fact about 55% rented and 45% owned. Thirty-four percent of Ridgeland residents over the age of 25 reported that they had earned a high school diploma. Almost 16% of respondents reported that they had at least some college education. Less than 10% of Ridgeland's residents had earned an Associates Degree or higher.

Most residents in Ridgeland are married, about 64%. Thirteen-percent of respondents reported that they were never married, twelve percent were widowed and 6 percent were divorced. Almost 90% of Ridgeland residents were born in the U.S., 90% of the foreign-born are of Latin American ancestry. As of 2000, most Ridgeland residents were working in service occupations, construction, extraction and maintenance, or sales and office occupations. On average, Ridgeland residents earn about $28,000 per year. About 20% of Ridgeland residents live below the poverty line.

On average, about half of homes in Ridgeland are valued at no less than $50,000 and no more than $99,999. Over half of homeowners have a mortgage with most paying between $300 and $999 per month, the same is true for renters. One average, about half of Ridgeland residents that rent, pay between $300 and $999 a month. For homeowners, their mortgage represents 15% of their total income whereas for many renters, their monthly housing expenses represent at least 30% of their income.

Alexander "Al" Norton's family's history parallels the changes that occurred in this small town considered by some to be "The Heart of the Low Country." His family owned and operated a farm. They lived in poverty, as did many of their neighbors. The Norton's, unlike many other blacks then and now were landowners. The manner in which Al Norton's family came to acquire the land is interesting and rooted in America's most peculiar institution, slavery.

Slavery was alive and well in many places in the U.S., including in South Carolina. Like many people of African ancestry living in the U.S. today, Norton is a descendent of slaves. He recalls being told the following:

Alexander Norton: My father's grandmother was named, Ma Becca. She was a slave. The slave master raped her. The lady she worked for gave her some money and sent her away.

Much has been written about the treatment of women during antebellum America, both free and enslaved, both black and white. The first group of people of African ancestry to settle in the U.S. likely arrived in 1619 and may have been indentured servants. The emerging U.S. economy relied on black, white, and Native American indentured servants until shifting to an economy based almost exclusively on slave labor. Indentured servants would perform labor on behalf of an individual or company for a prescribed time period. At the end of the service, the individual would be free and might also be given some land. This was the case until the 1640s. At this time, laws began to reflect the creation of a racialized social system. The sentencing of John Punch, a runaway indentured servant provides evidence of this historic transition. John Punch and several white indentured servants ran away to escape the harsh treatment they faced as indentured servants. Unfortunately, the men were captured. The white men received a punishment that was noticeably different than the punishment that John Punch, the only black male in the group, received. The white men had their years of service extended and were whipped. John Punch was not only whipped but he was also sentenced to a life of servitude.

Around this time, various laws were also passed determining the status of children born to those in bondage. As early as the 1660s, it was determined in the courts that the status of a child would follow the status of the mother. In other words, if a mother was born free then her offspring would be born free. Conversely, if a child was born to a woman in bondage then the child would be in bondage too. Dorothy Roberts (1997) has written eloquently and elaborately about efforts to control the reproductive freedom of blacks in her book, <u>Killing the Black Body</u>. She adds that the status of the father was for all intents and purposes irrelevant. Therefore, slave owners had an economic incentive to control black reproduction. This was evidenced in slave breeding and in non-consensual relations between the enslaved and their owners, particularly in the case of enslaved black women and their white slave owners.

Moreover, Roberts (1997) and others have shown that in the 1600s and for many years after that, it was not possible, legally to rape a slave. Yet the wife of a slave owner could obtain a divorce in a court of law on the grounds that her husband had relations with an enslaved woman. Slave narratives and the various hues that can be found in black families to this day provide support for the assertion that sexual relationships between the enslaved and their owners was not uncommon. Alexander Norton's family history provides further evidence.

> **Alexander Norton**: Ma Becca used the money and brought 350 acres of land.

The land purchased by Ma Becca was divided among her ancestors and was used to enrich community-at-large. Historical records show that John Norton, Sam Norton, and James Young purchased 15 acres of land in 1882 on behalf of the church the Norton family established, St. Mathews Baptist Church.

A portion of the land went to Norton's grandmother who then gave the land to her son, Willie, Alexander Norton's father. Although, Alexander's father worked in local log mill for more than 40 years, he along with his wife and children managed a farm. The

38

family's hard work helped supplement the $6 a week he earned at the mill. Norton reflects upon life on the family farm.

> **Alexander Norton**: My mother worked the farm. We used to plant corn, cucumbers, cantaloupes, okra, peas, and beans. We had a man that used to live with us. He worked on the farm with us and he would go home on the weekend. People would come in busloads and pick string beans and cotton.

Norton says that he learned a lot from working on the farm and from going to town with his mother. He learned valuable lessons that he would use to develop what becomes a million dollar business. Of his mother Norton says:

> **Alexander Norton**: She took care of that farm. We would go to town twice a week in the wagon to sell. She was a Cherokee Indian from Clakson, Georgia. She would go house-to-house. We would go with her too. We used to walk through the little town. She made a white sack for me and my sister and my brother and we would sell by the quarter. Then she would give us a quarter.

Norton's family was surrounded by black landowners.

> **Alexander Norton:** Most of my neighbors growing up were farmers. We were never sharecroppers. My cousins, my father's sisters, and my uncle, all live next store to us. We ran my aunts farm for her because she was a widow. My father had a few sisters and then he had the one brother. There were poor people in our community but we always shared a lot of things. People would come and help us. My father had his own sugar cane mill. We had a lot of potatoes. We had a lot of stuff to sell. We sold peanuts. We sold a lot of peanuts. We sold them for 10 cents a cup. My father brought a truck in 1951 with the money he earned selling peanuts!

Official records reveal how much the family had and what the family had to do to meet its basic needs. Willie Norton filed a number of documents entitled, Note and Mortgage. A note represents a promise to pay a given sum of money according a set of terms agreed upon by the individuals involved. The terms usually include mention of an interest rate, amount of principal and interest payments, payment due date and the repayment period. A mortgage, on the other hand, involves the pledge of property, sometimes a home, as security for repayment. Once a loan is paid the mortgage is satisfied.

In May 1926, for example, Norton's grandmother filed a Note and Mortgage document to settle a debt in the amount of $78.50, putting up five acres of what she describes as a "cotton plantation," the equivalent of about $927, at 8% interest. A year later, specifically in February 1927, Norton's grandmother transferred real estate to Al's father.

On December 21, 1936, Willie Norton filed another document promising to pay $80. He put up one black mare mule named Maude about 10 years old and one dark red milk cow with horns about 3 years old, with all increase. About a year later Norton completed a Note and Mortgage for $4,452, the equivalent of $65,000 adjusting for inflation. He put up a total of 26 acres including 8 acres of cotton.

Willie Norton completed at least 3 notes in 1946 totaling $655 or about $7,000 in contemporary dollars. He would again promise his family's mules and a horse to cover the debt. A year later, Willie Norton would put up a black mare, two cows and two calves in a promise to pay $175 ($1,500 in contemporary dollars). Two new wagon wheels were among the items put up to cover a promise to pay in the amount of $2,800, ($24,000 in contemporary dollars.) By 1950, Willie Norton owned $135 to ER Langford and offered up one mare and one heifer with horns. Five years later, he agrees to pay $343.30 ($2,700 in 2007 dollars) to Perry-Jones Company. To secure the payment he offer one dark red

mare mule about 10 years old, named Dollie; one one-horse Hickory wagon; one dark red milk cow with black spots with horns, his crop of cotton, corn, and beans planted or to be planted in 1955 on his land and lands of Okeetee Club in Jasper County.

According to the University of South Carolina, Okeetee Club is one of the largest hunting preserve in Jasper County. At about 48,000 acres, Okeetee Club organized in 1894. John Garnett built the original house. The house was destroyed by fire in the late 1950s but was rebuilt. According to 1970s estimates, about 1,000 acres are planted in corn, oats and feed for quails. Originally, the club was private and had twenty-one members. As a rule, club members could not sell their shares for more than they had paid for it, which resulted in the shares being passed down from one generation to the next. Today there are about 17 members remaining.

Ridgeland, South Carolina, from Alexander Norton's perspective was a community where black landowners lived among black sharecroppers. Nonetheless, the people cared for and shared with one another. It was also a community where racism was alive and well. However, according to Norton and his family did not encounter the type intimidation, indifference, and violence than many black families in the 1940s and the 1950s experienced in Ridgeland and beyond.

> **Alexander Norton:** Racism was bad. It was a big problem but no one ever bothered us. My father always taught us to be respectable and he taught us how to keep ourselves out of trouble. We didn't have to go to white people for nothing. They used to come to us. We used to sell to them. My mother and father never bothered anybody. There was prejudice. Oh my God, there was prejudice!

While Norton did not comment on any personal attacks on him or his family as a youngster growing up in the segregated South, he did comment on the manifestation of institutionalized racism as evidenced in the different experiences of black and white children at this time.

> **Alexander Norton**: As kids we had to walk to school. We walked 5 miles to school. Sometimes we wouldn't get to school until 10:00 in the morning. We didn't get any buses. The whites had buses. We had to walk and they would try and run us off the road. We ever had a new book in school. A truck would come and dump books and the teachers would go through them. Pages were torn out of the books; it was terrible.

It was not only racism that hindered Norton's educational pursuits, but it was also his father's attitude about school especially as it related to his male children.

> **Alexander Norton**: I was left back in first, second, and third grades. My father used to stop the boys from going to school. The girls would go. That is why my sister has a Masters degree and was a teacher in the 40s. She went to college.

Despite his father's belief that his boys belonged on the farm and not in the books, Norton always held schooling in very high esteem. He remembers always having a talent and an affinity for working with his hands and for math. These talents, which he discovered early on in life, would prove profitable in the future.

> **Alexander Norton**: I was always had a gift for math and for building things. My teacher used to tell me that he was afraid to give me math work because I was up to high school mathematics. I got straight A's in math that always stuck with me.

Despite Norton's love for math, it was his love for building things and his entrepreneurial spirit that would lead him to leave his boyhood home.

> **Alexander Norton:** My father always used to beat me for using his saw, because he told me not to use it. One time, I build a table and I sold it to a guy for $2.61. My father wanted the money. My mother said that his was not getting the money. So, I had to give him half.

Tensions between Alexander Norton and his father reached their climax when Alexander was 14.

> **Alexander Norton:** When I was 14 years old, my father beat me because the horse backed into the shaft. My mother told him I could make a shaft but I still got a beating. I ran away from home then. I had actually been planning the trip for about 2 years. I saved up the money that my mother would give us. I used some of the money to purchase a footlocker and one day I asked my mother for my bankbook. I did not tell her where I was going. I had $32 and I left Ridgeland headed for Miami. I figured I could have it better. My father didn't send us to school. We were working on the farm. We asked him for money and he would only give us a penny. I figure I could do better because I had a vision. I figured if I could go to Florida, I could do better.

Alexander Norton evaluated his options, as do many migrants. He, along with others who make the choice to uproot themselves from their place of birth, chose to relocate to a place where he already had family, Miami, Florida. Florida has long been home to many African-Americans. When most Americans think about slavery in America states like Mississippi, Alabama, Virginia, and South Carolina may come to mind, but few associated Florida with enslavement in America.

Scholars like Darlene Clark Hine have researched black communities in Florida during slavery. Slavery in this territory was much different than slavery in other parts. People of African ancestry were brought to the Florida during the 16th, 17th, and 18th centuries. According to Hine and others, these individuals and their descendents learned Spanish and many became Catholic while similar individuals in the British colonies became Protestants.

There were also greater opportunities for the enslaved in Florida to gain freedom than there were for their counterparts in the British colonies and elsewhere. Plantation agriculture was not as significant in Florida as in the British colonies. St. Augustine, which was established by the Spanish monarchy, was considered a military post. As a result, the number of enslaved peoples in Florida remained relatively small. Black men, for example, were more likely to serve as soldiers than workers in the field. Black slaves in Florida gained greater social status than black slaves elsewhere because of their military service and membership in the Catholic Church. Florida was home to one of the most sustainable maroon communities. Maroon is a term used to refer to slaves that escaped. Many of these individuals established their own settlements and were found in the Spanish colony of Florida. In fact in 1693, Hines et al 2006, reveals that the Spanish monarchy made the colony a refuge for those escaping slavery in the British colonies. Spain maintained a stronghold in this area until the mid-18th century went the British took control. Many of the people of African ancestry and the white residents of St. Augustine left for Cuba. Plantation slavery grew under British leadership.

Florida has been home to a substantial black population ever since. Decades before Al Norton decided to make Florida his home, Florida saw one of the nation's worst race riots. Racial tensions throughout the U.S. were high following the end of slavery in America. Between 1900 and 1930, racial tensions were at their peak. The nation saw violent clashes between blacks and whites in places like Atlanta, Springfield, East St. Louis, Houston, Chicago, Elaine, Tulsa and Rosewood.

Race riots broke out in Rosewood in 1923. Rosewood, Florida was a predominately black community. On New Year's Day, a white married woman named

Fannie Taylor who lived in an adjacent town said that a black man raped and beat her. Some whites in the town quickly assumed that Jesse Hunter, a black male resident of Rosewood, had done it. Still others contended that no rape or other assault had taken place at all. Rather, Fannie Taylor had made up the story so people would not know about her illicit extra-marital affair.

A group of white men, looking for revenge, went looking for Jesse. When they could not find him they attacked Aaron Carrier, another black male resident of the town. Carrier, it is believed, helped Fannie Taylor's lover escape. Other blacks in the town like Samuel Carter were shot and likely tortured. After these attacks, racial tensions between the two groups grew. Three days later a mob of angry white women entered Rosewood.

The black residents of Rosewood were no doubtful fearful of the white men, but they nonetheless were prepared. Black residents armed themselves ready to defend their families and their properties. Many had gathered at the home of Sylvester and Sarah Carrier, leaders of the resistance. The mob arrived at the Carrier home, fired upon the house killing Sarah. The blacks returned fire killing two white men who were attempting to gain entrance into the home. Reports indicated that the shooting lasted another day.

By January 6, 1923, a mob of about 250 people from nearby Gainesville, entered Rosewood, destroying the community. Most residents sought refuge in the wood areas following the place they and their families had called home and few ever looked back.

Florida, in the 1950s, when Alexander Norton arrived was a somewhat different place. Much had changed but in other ways, much had remained the same. Rose (1988) examined the black and Cuban communities in Miami over the past few decades. He contends that blacks were at this time marginalized especially in their economy of the urban South. Traditional black residential enclaves did exist in the 1950s like, Overtown and "Central Negro District," but would be reduced by the 1960s due to the demolition of housing for high ways and for other public works projects. The Liberty City-Brownsville district nearby did not fare much better. Portes and Stepick (1993) show that blacks were historically used by whites as unskilled laborers. They were residentially segregated into inferior neighborhoods that isolated them from whites and others. Reflecting up his time in Miami Norton recalls,

> **Alexander Norton**: In Miami, I went to school. I went to Booker T. Washington. My aunt had 3 children. I told her I would quit school and work. I worked for her husband. He gave me $2 a day. He cut grass. He was gardener. Then I got a job in the night and my aunt's husband starting giving me $20 a day. He had been taking advantage of me.

Norton was the first of his siblings to leave his childhood home. His brother would leave later at the age of 20 after enlisting in the Navy. A sister left after she got finished high school and got married.

> **Alexander Norton**: It was uncommon for 14-year old boys to leave home where I was from.

He stayed in Miami for a year and a half. Ironically, the very person that drove him away from home brought him back.

> **Alexander Norton:** My father got killed on the job so I returned to help my mother. I ran the farm and I helped raise my 3 brothers and my sister. I helped on the farm for 2 years. My mother got married again and my stepfather ran the farm and figured I would go to Brooklyn, New York and make some money to send back home.

CHAPTER 3

MOVIN' ON UP

Alexander Norton, like many blacks both past and present, left the South for what they thought would be greener pastures in the North. Fortunately for Norton, the choice turned out to be good one, but early on it did not seem that way. Norton decided to make New York his home on the advice of a friend that he went to school with in South Carolina who had already made the exodus northward. His friend, Philip Morris, told him that he could get a good job making $350 a week! Norton laughs today as he reflects upon how optimistic he was about the prospect of making such great money and the disappointment he ultimately felt when the job Morris talked about was nonexistent. Still Norton says that he has no regrets. His success in New York, tells us why.

Many others, before and after, Morris and Norton left the South. Much has been written about migration, about black migration in particular. Stewart Tolnay is among many scholars to write about the historic migration of blacks. He describes the Great Migration as a sharp increase in the northward migration of southern blacks during and after World War I, particularly during and after World War II[2].

---

[2] Source: http://www.uic.edu/educ/bctpi/greatmigration2/dataviewer/usa/USAleftcolumn.html

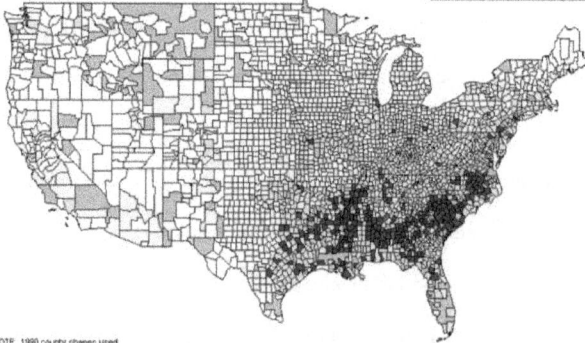

1910 African American population

Source: U.S. Census, Historical Census Data web site

1910 African American population by county

- 50,000 to 100,000 (7)
- 10,000 to 50,000 (277)
- 1,000 to 10,000 (731)
- 100 to 1,000 (826)
- 0 to 100 (1163)
- No data (0)

NOTE: 1990 county shapes used
Approximately 90% of historical counties represented

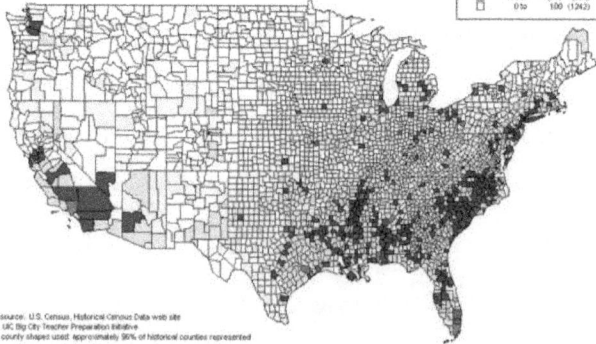

1960 African American population

1960 African American population by county

- 500,000 to 1,000,000 (2)
- 100,000 to 500,000 (28)
- 50,000 to 100,000 (29)
- 10,000 to 50,000 (306)
- 1,000 to 10,000 (919)
- 100 to 1,000 (598)
- 0 to 100 (1242)

Data source: U.S. Census, Historical Census Data web site
Map: UIC Big City Teacher Preparation Initiative
1990 county shapes used; approximately 90% of historical counties represented

In the article, The Great Migration and the Changes in the Northern Black Family, 1940-1990, Tolnay shows that the primary motivation was economic. Factories in the North expanded production and did so rapidly to meet materials needs related to fighting the war. This led to an increased demand for workers. At the same time, access to relatively cheap immigrant labor was limited as the supply began to shrink. Hostilities in Europe, recruitment of southern blacks, and historic changes in immigration laws during this period all contributed to the Great Migration. Lack of adequate opportunities in the South was another obvious factor.

Throughout much of the South's checkered past, blacks have found limited economic opportunities. Although Norton's family owned their own land, many other black families, particularly those in the rural South, were over represented among those with tenancy status. Most black men working as unskilled laborers and most black women worked as domestic servants. Some blacks, like preachers and teachers, representing albeit a smaller percentage of the southern black population than other blacks, did live quite well.

About 20 years before Alexander Norton was born, blacks began leaving the South. Tolnay found that between 1910 and 1930, the number of blacks living outside of the South increased. In 1910, 5% of southern-born blacks lived outside the region. By 1930, the number almost tripled. Black migration northward slowed during the Great Depression but increased again by the 1950s. By the 1950s, 20% of southern-born blacks were living outside of the region. Most blacks ventured either North or West.

Southern migrants like Norton often arrived in the North with a stigma attached. At the same time that Norton and others were arriving in the North, northern communities and black families in the North were undergoing profound changes. According to Tolnay, southern-born black migrants like Alexander Norton were often to blame. There were those who argued, among other things, that the migrants brought with them deviant family patterns. These patterns included desertion, pre-marital sexual relations, and out-of-wedlock births.

On the contrary, Tolnay was able to show that there wasn't any support for the argument that southern migrants came to the North with a family culture that was dysfunctional. Rather the migrants were more advantaged in that regard than many of their northern counterparts. Compared to northern-born blacks, Tolnay was able to show that southern-born blacks living in the North had higher rates of labor force participation, lower levels of unemployment, higher incomes, lower levels of poverty, and lower levels of welfare dependency.

Norton clearly possessed many characteristics of what Tolnay refers to as the migrant advantage. The work was not always glamorous, but he was a hard worker. Instead of the well paying job that he was expecting, Norton says this,

> **Alexander Norton:** I ended up getting a job as a dishwasher. My friend was a Machine Operator. When I got to New York he told me that his boss didn't need anybody so I washed dishes for $20 a week, six days a week.
>
> When I first came there I lived with my cousin. She had 5 kids. I told her that I wanted a room. She lived at 729 Green Avenue in Brooklyn, New York. She rented me a room for $6.

Street map of Brooklyn neighborhood where Norton settled. Source: oasiscitynyc.net

Two days after arriving in New York, Al Norton signed up to be a boxer.

> **Alexander Norton:** I met Otis Smith when I came to New York. He introduced me to Cus D'Amato, Floyd Paterson's manger. My dream, my goal, the only thing I wanted in life at that time was to be heavyweight champion. I met Floyd Paterson and Bill Paterson, his brother. Bill had a restaurant on Gates avenue. They were from North Carolina. He later became champion.
>
> I really wanted something out of life. I boxed for 3 years. I was a Golden Glove champion for 2 years. I turned professional. I fought on a Floyd Paterson card. I fought in Madison Square Garden. Against Archibald Terrell, I had a six round fight. Then I fought 7 or 8 professional fights and then I broke my right hand and ended my career.

Boxrec identifies several fights that Norton fought in for 1958 and 1959. Aside from the fight that took place in the Garden, Norton also fought in St. Nick arena and Montreal, Quebec, Canada. He fought the likes of Freddie Todino, Bartolo Sini, and Benito Favatto.

Constantine "Cus" D'Amato who Norton encountered at the gym, was a legend in boxing. D'Amato has been linked to a number of professional boxers and trainers including Floyd Paterson, Mike Tyson, Teddy Atlas, and Jose Torres. According to Lisa Scott of Boxing News, D'Amato, a Bronx native, was the son of Italian immigrants and himself had dreams of being a champion boxer. An injury to one of his eyes ended his personal career but the injury could do little to quell his love for boxing. During the same year that Alexander Norton was born, D'Amato co-founded Gramercy Gym in New York at 14th and Irving Place. He would eventually sell the gym for $1 and establish another in the Catskill region of New York State, a place that he would come to call home.

D'Amato's greatest success, some say, came with Floyd Paterson. Paterson would not only become a world champion but he would also become the first boxer to earn a million dollar purse. Paterson taught boxing at a reform school; was an Olympic gold medalist; for a time enjoyed the status of youngest heavyweight champion; and would become a two time heavyweight champion. Norton and Paterson developed a friendship that would last several decades. However, once Norton's boxing career officially ended, he joined the service.

Alexander Norton: In 1957, I went into the army. I was drafted. A lot of people were drafted then. I didn't mind being drafted. They did me a favor. I was stationed in Fort Dix, New Jersey. I loved it.

Norton and many of his peers did not volunteer to serve instead they were drafted. According to the Selective Service, the first peacetime draft in the U.S. was enacted in 1940. The enactment was in response to global tensions. After World War II, the draft expired only to be reenacted about to years later. The purpose of the reenactment of the draft was to ensure an adequate level of military force to combat the Cold War. Beginning in 1948 and lasting until the early 1970s, men were drafted to fill vacancies in the armed forces. The draft ended in 1973, but not everyone drafted remained in the service.

> **Alexander Norton:** They were letting a lot of men out of the service because of low IQ. I wanted to stay in. They let me go.
>
> That is what gave me drive. I was able to focus. I thought to myself---- if they think that I am too dumb to serve the U.S, I am going to prove them wrong by making something of myself!
>
> When I came out of the service I went to an employment agency. There was a black lady there. She said she would get me into school for free. She told me to bring my discharge papers.

With assistance, Norton was able to enroll in Brooklyn Tech. He went there for four years and studied carpentry. He learned how to read blueprints. Then he got a job working in a construction company.

> **Alexander Norton:** This guy taught me how to scale and how to read blueprints. This is what I was doing in school. Soon I was making $80 a week. Then my boss gave me a raise. School brought me from a dishwasher to over a million dollars a year!

Norton's decision to come to New York was paying off in a number of other ways. In addition to developing the skills that he would need to be successful worker, he was also developing important ties and networks that would assist him in becoming a property owner and successful businessman.

> **Alexander Norton:** While I was in Brooklyn, a guy and me went fishing on Long Island. He told me I should think about buying property there. This guy used to live on my block. He already owned property there.

Many places in the U.S. during the 1960s and the 1970s were becoming more diverse while others were becoming more segregated. Discrimination in housing was one of the factors that contributed to racial segregated communities in America during this time, including on Long Island.

Housing has been the battleground for racial conflicts in America because of the significance of housing to individuals, families, and communities. Housing is one of the most significant social and economic commodities in American society. The value of one's home comprises the largest part of the average American's portfolio. Some groups, including blacks have historically been left out of the home buying process, especially during the greatest housing boom in American history, which occurred in the early to middle part of the 20th century. At the same time, the housing boom became a means for white immigrants, many from Southern, Central and Eastern Europe to become not only home owners but to become "white" and to be viewed as American. Through discriminatory practices, those administered by the federal government, financial institutions, realtors and others, some racial and ethnic groups were systematically deterred or prohibited from owning a home. The recent documentary entitled, Race the Power of an Illusion: The House We Live In, provides a stunning analysis of the role that race has played in advantaging some groups while disadvantaging others, especially as it relates to the birth of American suburbs for whites and the birth of vertical ghettos for many others. Norton observed this as it happened on Long Island yet contends that things have changed somewhat. How and why such changes have taken place will be discussed later.

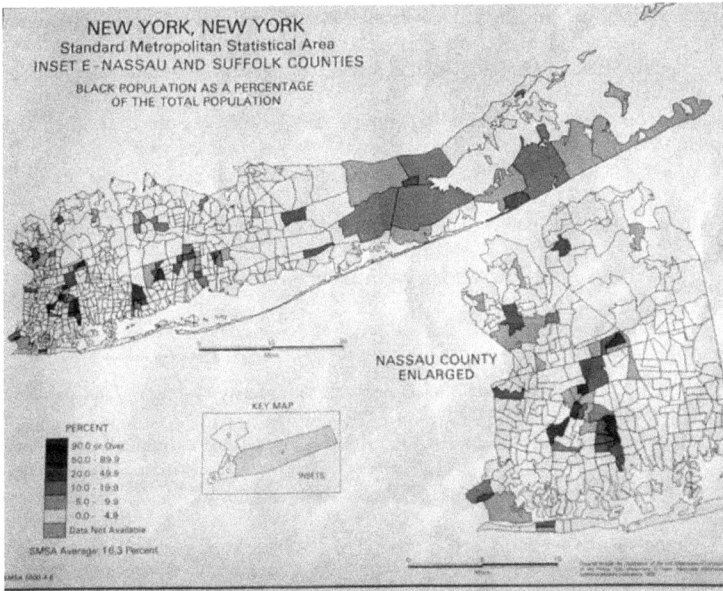

Source: http://www.sunysb.edu/libmap/img0051b.jpg

Despite efforts to address barriers to home ownership for racial and ethnic minority groups, racial and ethnic differences in home ownership as well as in housing values have persisted. Discrimination in mortgage lending and at other stages in the home buying process, has led to lower rates of home ownership among nonwhites and to lower returns on the housing investment for nonwhites relative to whites.

Racial differences in housing values have also been linked to racial differences in human capital and social capital. Blacks, it is argued have lower levels of education, occupational prestige and income and weaker social ties to networks and institutions that assist in the process of asset accumulation compared to whites. The fact that whites prefer to live, learn and work with other whites instead of with nonwhites, is one of the more prevailing theoretical perspectives used to explain racial and ethnic differences in human capital and social capital. Racial and ethnic differences in wealth, especially in the area of home ownership and housing values, have been examined in the context of the effectiveness, or lack thereof, of historic and contemporary social policies. Many scholars today argue that contemporary social policies should focus on bridging the racial and ethnic gap in asset ownership, particularly in the area of home ownership and housing values.

Racial differences in homeownership between blacks and whites have been observed historically due in part to efforts on the part of individuals as well as institutions to block access to this means of wealth accumulation for blacks. This was evident in the Home Owner's Loan Corporation (HOLC), which provided funds to people to avoid defaulting on their property as well as low interest loans to regain property that had already been lost.

The HOLC was established in the 1930s and has been critiqued by scholars for playing a central role in residential segregating racial and ethnic groups in America. Specifically, scholars such as Massey and Denton (1993) have contended and shown that through the use of color-coded maps for urban areas and the appraisals of housing characteristics for neighborhoods that the HOLC institutionalized racially based procedures for determining the suitability for mortgage loans which favored whites moving to the suburbs while disadvantaging who were largely in urban areas and kept out of the suburbs by those who feared that their mere presence would lead to instability and bring down property values. The procedures set by the HOLC, which remained in existence until the mid-1950s, served as a model for other financial institutions in America.

The HOLC "used red as the color code for neighborhoods with the lowest appraisals, and so redlining became not just an evocative term for categorizing communities, but also an empirical reality in the agency that pioneered the long-term, fully amortized mortgage presumably, the first concrete evidence of the racial bias in federal housing programs".

The Federal Housing Administration (FHA), also created in the 1930s and functioned independently of the HOLC administratively yet along with the HOLC helped finance military housing and homes for veterans and their families returning from the war in the 1940s. Prior to the creation of these two entities home ownership was out of reach for most. Prospective homebuyers could be financed for about half the value of the home, the loan had to be repaid within a relatively short period of time, namely five years with a large balloon payment at the end of the term. Most Americans in the early 1930s and 1940s did not have the economic resources to own their own homes and the U.S. was largely a nation of renters. The FHA and HOLC made home ownership less of a dream and more of a reality for some by making home ownership more accessible. Through the FHA and HOLC individuals could make a down payment equal to about 20% and have 20 to 30 years to pay off the loan. Risks to the lender and to the homebuyers were lowered. However, according to FHA underwriting handbook, "if a neighborhood is to retain stability, it is necessary that properties shall continue to be occupied by the same social and racial classes." This led to the exclusion of existing housing in cities where many blacks lived as a result of the Great Migration due to the fact these neighborhoods were in large part already heterogeneous, consequently this policy encouraged suburbanization. Moreover, the FHA found that single-family units were preferable to mixed-use housing, which placed further limitations on housing options for urban dwellers. This represented divestment in cities and in blacks for investments in suburbs and in whites as whites moved to the suburbs to take advantage of the affordable loans. Moreover, it has been shown that the FHA promoted racial covenants where whites would vow not to sell their homes to nonwhites.

Shelley v. Kramer (1948) banned the use of restrictive covenants but the practices of the FHA changed little. The federal government was reluctant to do anything of substance about housing discrimination so the practice persisted. Former President Kennedy issued a weak executive order in 1960 that was supposed to ban discrimination in housing. However the act exempted existing housing and newly constructed housing except where federal funding was involved. It was not until 1968 with the passage of the Fair Housing Law that discrimination was banned in all areas of the rental and sale of housing. The passage of the Fair Housing Act of 1968, some contend, lacked the enforcement needed to adequately deal with the ongoing discrimination in the sale and rental of housing in America.

Exclusion by the FHA meant that blacks were ineligible for the most affordable homes and thus were kept out of the housing boom that became an important source of equity and wealth generation, particularly for whites in America. In short, between 1940 and 1970, blacks were shut out of a historic period of housing construction and ownership through the continuation of discriminatory practices. Federal practices led to the creation and the maintenance of racial segregated neighborhoods. The practices prevented black homeownership and created inequalities in equity between black and whites for blacks fortunate enough to be homeowners in the first place.

Norton faced many obstacles in his efforts to become a homeowner on Long Island. He recalls the following:

> **Alexander Norton:** I brought a piece of property on Long Island for $1500. I was paying $40 a month. I had two years to pay it and I paid it before it ahead of time. I built a house on that property. I built it myself.
>
> My brother helped too. He came to live with us from down South. I made him go to school.

Norton built his home in Coram near Gordon Heights, a historic community on the island. Gordon Heights, according to Hofstra University, was specifically created for a black population. Evidence suggests that after emancipation, free blacks established communities around the island. Such communities include Sag Harbor, New Cassel, Roslyn Heights, Amityville, Glen Cove, and Bridgehampton. Other predominately black communities were established during the post-World War II era as a result of white flight. By the 1960s, some neighborhoods transitioned racially, from white to black in such places as Hempstead, Roosevelt, and Freeport.

A 1969 meeting at the community center in Gordon Heights, one of Long Island's -- and the nation's -- earliest developments marketed to blacks. (Newsday Photo, December 15, 2007).

Alexander Norton: I would go to Long Island on the weekends and lay blocks. It took me 2 ½ years because I used to make $80 a week. I used to keep $5 in my pocket and I'd give the rest to my wife.

My wife never worked at that time. I had a beautiful wife. We had three kids. She was from Alabama. We met in New York. I was eighteen years old and we went before the judge. Her grandmother signed for us. We got married by the Justice of the Peace.

Norton's first wife, Alcesta, died in a car accident in the 1990s in the rural upstate New York community she and her husband came to call home. A local park was named in her honor. Norton eventually remarried. He married Lucy Merriweather some years later.

Returning to the topic of how he built his first home, Norton says,

Alexander Norton: I was trying to get a mortgage as I was trying to build the house. I had 7 banks turn me down. I had the house ready to put the roof on. I needed $9,000. Every bank turned me down.

A man at a lumber company introduced me to a millionaire and he said he could get a loan for me, $9,000 over a 15-year period. I didn't want to put up with no long-term loan.

So, I turned to my wife, Alcesta, and told her I was going back to Brooklyn to buy an apartment house and I did that. I brought a four family apartment house.

I got the property from the owners of a real estate company that I did some work for back then. The owners used to give me small jobs. I used to install mailboxes and locks.

I told them that I was interested in buying some of their property. They were always complaining to me and to those around them that they weren't making any money off some of the houses they owned.

I explained how much I could pay a month. They seemed reluctant to sell to me at first. I made my case. I told them that they had a lot of houses and that I only wanted one. I asked if there was anyway we could work something out. I told them that I had $5,000 and they sold it to me.

I turned around and sold that house. I took the money I made off that house and I set up a separate checking account. In another month I went back and brought another one house from them. Each time I went back to them to purchase another house, I would ask them why they were holding on to the properties if they weren't making any money because each time they were hesitant to sell to me. Then I brought another house in 11 months. Then a year later I brought another apartment house.

I never lived in any of the apartment houses I brought. I rented them out. I had different people working on the plumbing and handing other jobs. I never met them. They were referred to me by the real estate business. I had four apartment houses.

By the time that I went into business for myself, I had 16 lots paid for! I got them from auctions. The properties were up for auction because of back taxes or because the person who owned the property died and did not leave a will. I was able to buy the properties with no money down. I would have 6 months to close. I would sell the property before the end of the 6-month period and then use the profits to buy more property.

I decided to go into business for myself because I had a vision. I believed that I could make more money working for myself than by working for someone else.

I named my first company, Al Construction. My lawyer said that if I build another house I would need to have another company to protect my personal finances. So I got incorporated and named the business, Black Bros. Building Corp.

CHAPTER 4

TURNING THE TABLES:
MAKING THE SYSTEM WORK FOR YOU

Al Norton decided to make the system work for him. He decided to use the skills that he had learned from going to town with his mother to sell crops; from managing the family farm; from studying at Brooklyn Tech; and from watching those around him to build what would become a million dollar business. Norton established Black Bros. Building Corp. on May 26, 1972 on Suffolk County, New York. How Norton came up with the company name and how that company became successful are interesting and revealing stories that get at the heart of the many challenges facing individuals and groups interested in forming and expanding businesses. As is the case with many business owners, both past and present, access to financial, social, and human capital served as barriers for Norton. Gaining access to government contracts, often seen as a potentially lucrative avenue especially for small minority-owned businesses. This too was a challenge, which Norton confronted and met.

Along with many others, including many blacks, in the 1970s, 1980s, and 1990s, Norton was interested in controlling his own economic destiny through business ownership. During this time period, the number of black-owned businesses grew more than U.S. businesses as a whole although blacks did not gain as much for their investment into business ownership as did others. Differences in the likelihood of business ownership for blacks relative to other groups and differences in the returns on investment into business ownership might be related to a number of factors including the concentration of black-owned businesses in selected industries, location, and discrimination.

Black owned-businesses are more likely to be in the service industry than any other industry. For example, the economic census conducted by the U.S. Census Bureau found in 1992, 1997, 2002, and in 2007 that more than half of all black businesses were in the service industry. This industry may not yield the same receipt levels as businesses in other industries, which might be more lucrative. Far fewer black businesses are in the construction industry typically, less than 10% were in construction. Retail trade was the second most common industry type for black businesses.

Location might also impact the viability of business in general and black-owned businesses in particular. For example, the areas with the largest black populations are among the areas with the largest number of black-owned businesses. Los Angeles-Long Beach, CA and New York, NY have among the largest black populations and they routinely top the list of metropolitan statistical areas with the largest numbers of black-owned firms.

In addition to industry type and location, discrimination is another factor that influences business ownership, propelling some individuals into business ownership while pushing others away. Individuals who face discrimination in the labor force, for instance, may opt for self-employment and/or business ownership. Such a move often allows individuals to reap the rewards associated with employment in what is referred to as the primary sector.

In the primary sector, individuals earn what are thought to be fair and decent wages. They have a relatively high level of job security and fringe benefits when compared with others. Those kept out of the primary sector might find themselves marginalized in the secondary sector. Unlike the primary sector, jobs opportunities in the secondary sector are characterized as dead end, low wage jobs, with little or no benefits. Racial and ethnic minorities and women tend to be over represented in the secondary sector. Members of these disadvantaged groups may view business ownership as their only vehicle for attaining the often elusive American Dream as measured by the tangible effects of employment in the primary sector. Since blacks are among the most disadvantaged groups in the U.S., it is expected that they would have among the highest levels of business ownership yet blacks have among the lowest rates suggesting that the pathway to black business ownership differs from other groups.

Norton's pathway to business ownership was in the construction industry. Construction can be a very challenging industry type especially for minority-owned businesses. However, a lot of construction was occurring on Long Island in the early 1970s and Norton wanted to capitalize on his knowledge and skills. Norton was contracted to do a number of jobs when his business was first getting started. He paved driveways, built new homes, and helped to repair and modify existing homes. However, he longed to include government contracts in his growing portfolio of new and repeat clients. For Norton and apparently for many others, government contracts were hard to come by.

According to Norton, there were concerns from many in the community that such contracts were not being awarded to minorities. Research supports Norton's observation that minority businesses have historically and even in contemporary times, faced hurdles in securing government contracts. A study from the Urban Institute entitled, "Do Minority-Business Owners Get a Fair Share of Government Contracts," contends that minority businesses have not historically received their fair share of government contracts and this is due in part or in whole to barriers that minority businesses, especially face, in two key areas. The first area is related to the formation and growth of businesses. The second area concerns government contracting.

Minority business owners have difficulties forming and expanding their businesses because they tend to have limited access to financial, social, and human capital and to the broader market than others. For example, blacks are less likely to have assets that help them form and grow their businesses; this reflects their limited access to financial capital. A fairly recent report finds that accessing financial capital through conventional means, i.e. banks, may be easier at some institutions than for others:

GREENLINING INSTITUTE'S REPORT CARD[3]

SBA Lending (Dollar Amount)

Top Two for African Americans

1. Bank of America $24,288,800

2. JPMorgan Chase $13,123,600

Top Two for All Minorities

1. Bank of America $176,680,100

2. Comerica $146,247,800

Bottom Two for African Americans

13. Fifth Third Bancorp $1,819,848

14. Wachovia Corp. $1,810,000

Bottom Two for All Minorities

13. BB&T Corp. $10,337,000

14. Wachovia Corp. $6,991,150

---

[3] Townes, Glenn. 2005. "Report reveals best lenders for black business: findings lead to renewed calls for public analysis of SBA loans." Black Enterprise.

GREENLINING INSTITUTE'S REPORT CARD[4]

SBA Lending (Percentage of Loans)

Top Two for African Americans

1. M&T Banking Corp.   8.3%

2. BB&T Corp.   7.2%

Top Two for All Minorities

1. HSBC USA Inc.   49.0%

2. Bank of America   40.0%

Bottom Two for African Americans

13. Wells Fargo   2.6%

14. Fifth Third Bancorp 2.2%

Bottom Two for All Minorities

13. National City Corp. 13.0%

14. Fifth Third Bancorp 9.0%

---

[4] Townes, Glenn. 2005. "Report reveals best lenders for black business: findings lead to renewed calls for public analysis of SBA loans." Black Enterprise.

Prospective black business owners not only face limited access to financial capital but to social capital too. They are less like to have the social ties and networks that members of the majority group and other minority groups have that help promote the formation and growth of businesses. These social ties and social networks referred to here constitute indicators of social capital. Research reveals that blacks have less social capital than members of the dominant group and are not able to reap benefits by exploiting their unique racial and ethnic qualities as some other groups have done in a number of ethnic enclaves and communities throughout the country, such as in the case of Cubans in Miami.

Additionally, blacks have on average, lower levels of professional training and other indicators of human capital that serve as barriers to business ownership. The inability of many black businesses because many tend to be relatively small in size to compete in the open market limits their opportunities for success. Some have argued that black business development was more viable under the oppressive system of Jim Crow in America.

Fortunately for Norton, he was able to face the challenges associated with having limited access to financial, social and human capital in a number of ways. Additionally, he was able to procure a number of government contracts and compete in the competitive Suffolk County market. Overcoming the obstacles Norton faced must have seemed insurmountable at first. To begin his climb upward, Al Norton had to get his business noticed. He and other minority business owners felt like they were invisible in the 1970s. Norton states,

Alexander Norton: There was a lot of construction on Long Island when I started my business. People were complaining that minorities were not being hired to do the work. The government had in the paper that they could not find any minorities to do the work, so I named my company Black Bros. Building Corp that way there would be no mistake, they could let their fingers do the walking!

Getting the attention of government officials is not the only barrier Norton and other black business owners face. The Urban Institute study found that government contracts tend to be so large at times those black businesses that are relatively small cannot compete for contracts with bigger businesses that, are more likely to be owned by members of the majority group. If the contracts were broken down small firms, including black owned firms could compete more successfully. Moreover, the Urban Institute demonstrated that some government agencies have waived requirements calling for a predetermined number of minority contractors in favor of majority contractors, which might also be responsible for limiting access to government contracts for minority owned businesses. Moreover, the report contended that in the absence of effective screening, members of the majority group put up a false minority front. Also, notices of available government contracts were often limited and members of majority group owned businesses had a tendency to under bid black and other minority owned businesses. Despite efforts on the part of government to address these barriers inequalities related to the procurement of government contracts lives on. In fact, the institute revealed that minority business owners received about $.57 for every dollar they were expected to receive in government contracts.

The report considered a number of industries, revealing that disparities in the number of dollars actually awarded and the number of dollars expected to be awarded, were greatest in Goods, and Other Services, while fewer disparities were fewer in Professional Services and Construction. Parity was almost reached in the Construction Subcontracting industry.

Overtime, Al Norton's construction company, Black Bros Building Corp was able to secure government contracts. He credits his ability to secure contracts to effective advertising. He advertised in local newspapers and on his growing fleet of trucks. His business grew also through referrals and word of mouth. He built up a reputation in the community as a trusted entrepreneur that proved beneficial. Norton secured contracts with the town of Brookhaven, Longwood High School, Brookhaven National Laboratory, State University of New York, Stony Brook (SUNY Stony Brook), a local firehouse and Brookwood, a housing complex.

The town of Brookhaven, one of Norton's biggest clients, is larger than many major cities including Atlanta and Miami. The town of Brookhaven includes such villages and hamlets as Bellport, Coram, Gordon Heights, Middle Island, Shirley and Stony Brook. Today, it is home to about 400,000 residents and contains some 2,000 miles of roadway many of which Norton and his crew worked on.

Black Bros Building Corp also did work at Longwood High School. Norton's sons, nephews, nieces, and neighbors attended the school. After procuring the contracts his company was responsible for a number of projects including the athletic track. Norton developed such an attachment to the school and to the community that his company established a competitive, college scholarship for graduating seniors. His company gave thousands of dollars to young scholars many of whom went on to prestigious institutions of higher learning and to careers in medicine and education, to name a few. Norton recalls meeting several of the scholarship recipients who expressed their gratitude for the financial support they received from Black Bros Building Corp.

Brookhaven National Laboratory and SUNY Stony Brook are two of the largest institutions on Long Island and two institutions that entrusted work at their facilities to Black Bros Building Corp. Brookhaven National Laboratory, according to the lab's official web page, is one of ten national laboratories. It is funded primarily funded by the Office of Science of the U.S. Department of Energy. The lab conducts research in the physical, biomedical, and environmental sciences. Additionally, it conducts research in energy technologies and national security. Brookhaven Lab also builds and operates major scientific facilities available to university, industry and government researchers.

Among the universities that utilize the laboratory is SUNY Stony Brook. Stony Brook is a top rated university, offering a quality education to more than 25,000 students each year.

Al Norton's success did not happen over night. He had big dreams but he took incremental steps.

> **Alexander Norton:** When I started, I hired one guy. Then I hired another guy. I did not rely on the business completely at first. I continued to work for someone while I was growing my business. I was making about $500 a week from my job and about $150 a week from my business.
>
> I decided that I wanted to build my business. I know that I would have to put more people to work and expand. So I decided to get on the local auction list. I started buying property that had been seized due to backed taxes.

I would go to the bank every year and a get a $3,000 loan. I would use that money to buy a piece of property. I would pay the bank off and then I would buy another piece. I had 16 lots paid for in three years and I knew then that I was really ready for business.

Not all new businesses are as successful as Norton's business would become. Norton was in business for more than 20 years. To what does he attribute his success? How did Black Bros Building Corp become one of the first black owned construction companies to be bonded in Suffolk County, an honor that won he recognition from the local branch of the National Association for the Advancement of Colored People (NAACP)?

Many government contracts include a bonding requirement, which can serve as an obstacle to prospective business owners. According to the U.S. Department of Labor, the statutory requirement states, "Every officer, agent, shop steward, or other representative or employee of any labor organization (other than a labor organization whose property and annual financial receipts do not exceed $5,000 in value), or a trust in which a labor organization is interested, who handles funds or other property thereof shall be bonded to provide protection against loss by reason of acts of fraud or dishonesty on his part directly or through connivance with others."

Bonding is defined by the Department of Labor as an insurance agreement. The agreement essentially guarantees repayment for financial loss. The loss might be caused to the covered organization by an act or failure to act of a third person. The purpose of bonding is to protect the financial operations of companies and unions from losses caused by acts of fraud or dishonesty by officers, employees, or other representatives. The Department of Labor asserts that there are variations in the types of bonds.

"A bond may be either individual, schedule, or blanket.

An individual bond is a single bond that covers one named person for a designated amount.

A schedule bond covers either named individuals or specific positions or offices. Typically, a name schedule bond lists named individuals and covers them separately for a designated amount, while a position schedule bond lists specific positions, covers each for a designated amount, and covers any persons who may occupy any such position during the term of the bond.

A blanket bond covers all officers and employees of an insured union or trust, but without a schedule or list of those covered; all new officers and employees are covered automatically as well as officers and employees whose duties change to include handling funds.

Acceptable blanket bonds may operate on either an aggregate or multiple penalty bases. A blanket bond on an aggregate penalty basis provides for recovering the same amount regardless of whether a loss is caused by one person or by several persons acting together. For example, if a union has a blanket bond for $10,000 on an aggregate penalty basis and two officers or employees are involved jointly in the embezzlement of $20,000, only $10,000 could be recovered from the surety company for the embezzlement.

A blanket bond on a multiple penalty basis provides separate coverage for each person. For example, if a union has a blanket bond on a multiple penalty basis and two officers or employees are involved jointly in the embezzlement of $20,000, the full $20,000 could be recovered because $10,000 could be recovered for each individual."[5]

Paul King, author of "Can You Dig It? Affirmative Action and African Americans in the Construction Industry,"[6] contends that bond companies have played a significant role in discriminating against blacks. King should know, he has been involved

---

[5] Source: http://www.dol.gov/esa/regs/compliance/olms/bonding.htm#b

[6] In Motion Magazine February 6, 1999.

in the construction field for decades and has undoubtedly encountered a number of boding companies. In fact, he asserts that he was a driving force behind the 1969 shut down of construction sites in Chicago. He along with a host of others shut down the cites to protest the absence of black contractors and workers for building projects supported by funds from the U.S. Department of Housing and Urban Development (HUD). The group of protestors according to King was encouraged by an executive order that compelled contractors working on federally funded projects to end discrimination against blacks and to engage in actions that would increase the number of black workers and contactors. King concludes that far more advances have been made in requiring individuals and companies to take "affirmative action" in addressing discrimination in employment, education and political districting than in the construction industry over time.

Hence, it can be state that the restrictive practices of bond companies and banks have hindered blacks in the construction industry. This along with discrimination by unions and trade unions placed blacks at a severe disadvantage and hurt their ability to establish and to grow thriving businesses. Unfortunately, the trend persists. Deception, ignorance and greed, adds King, continue to be at the root of the problem. These three elements were not well suited to Norton's worldview of business philosophy, however.

Norton offers the following advice on becoming successful in business,

Alexander Norton: You have to be serious, sincere, and fair to all people. You have to be honest.

Spirituality is an important ingredient in any recipe for success in business and in life for Norton.

Alexander Norton: You have to take God with you. God doesn't want us to look back but to look forward. He reminds us that whatever has happened in the past, we should just let it go and not look back. I asked God once, why my business was not growing like I wanted it to grow. Why couldn't I have a big business? I understood then that just because my business was not as big as I wanted it to be then that didn't mean that it wouldn't be in the future.

So I started devoting more time to my business, about half of my time went into Black Bros. Building Corp. Soon, I had 20 guys working for me and I had contracts with the State, local schools, the town.... I grew to have over 850 customers a year.

I would always guarantee my work. I would not take any money until the job was done. You can't cheat people. Your work should reflect truth and dignity.

Any man that goes into business can make it. If a business owner is dishonest, his business is likely to fail. It is just not going to work.

By having faith and by increasing his access to financial, social, and human capital, Al Norton was able to form and expand a successful enterprise. Yet in doing so, he experienced discrimination, much like the discrimination that other minority business have experienced and unfortunately continue to experience. Norton contends however that discrimination does not account for all of disparity that exists between minorities and others, especially between blacks and whites.

Alexander Norton: We hold ourselves back. You know why? I'm going to tell you a big reason. We came from a people that taught us the right way. They taught us morals. They taught us to have respect, but we let the system take our pride away. We hear the words, but we don't let it work for us.

Our ministers, leaders and parents taught us the right way to live. They instilled in us the idea that we don't do anything on our own. They reminded us that when God created us, he created something very special.

They encouraged us to walk in faith, to believe that God was in control that he was in charge of our lives. We were to always walk in the authority that we have as children of God. Parents are not teaching their children these values, these morals today. Now the kids are trying to buck the system.

Norton adds,

> **Alexander Norton:** You have to learn the system and let the system work for you. Living in the U.S., you have as much right as anyone else to live or to own a business even in areas where you may not be welcomed.

> If I want to live any place in the U.S. I will even if I have to shoot myself in at night and shoot my way out in the morning! That is my right. We have to claim it.

> We only deserve to have what we are supposed to have. If you walk in faith and stand up for your rights then things come to you. Again you have to understand the system and let system work for you. If you buck against the system then you'll be in the headlines of garbage.

The garbage that Norton is referring to includes the myriad of news reports that we read about or see on the evening news about young people, especially young black men. Some of these young men decide to use illegal means to obtain wealth, status, and power. Blacks like so many in the U.S. have been overwhelmed by materialism and individualism and the headlines are filled with people from various racial and ethnic groups, including blacks, trying to find the shortcut to the American Dream, contends Norton. These two core values are negatively impacting blacks and others. According to Norton, it is one of the things keeping some minorities from being success in business and in life.

> **Alexander Norton:** Some of us are too preoccupied with keeping up with the latest styles. We pick up garbage. We as a people, used to walk and talk with dignity. We knew how to present ourselves. We knew how to

dress and how to show respect for ourselves and for others. Without these things, you can't get anywhere in life. I don't care how much education you got, if you got a nasty personality, you can forget it! You have to be humble.

This is the only country where you can come from a dishwasher to over a millionaire!

Al Norton is not the first to raise concerns about the current generation and the apparent obsession of some with material gain and loathe for hard work. Hip-hop culture is often the scapegoat and cited by many as the reason for the growth of materialism and individuals among the latest generation. It has been blamed for distorting black manhood, disrespecting women, and destroying the overall moral fiber of many young people, especially young black youth. Norton believes that the blame lies however at the feet of some parents and their failure to communicate those things, which used to be held in a much higher regard.

Norton finds as many others do that far too many youth fail to set goals for themselves and work within the system to put their visions for themselves, for their families, and for their communities, into action. The issue of course did not originate with hip-hop culture nor does one group or subpopulation have a monopoly on individualism and materialism.

Michael Eric Dyson, noted scholar argues that the nation as a whole celebrates materialism. [7] Peter Skerry questions whether or not growing individualism among blacks

---

[7] See "Extend King's legacy by aiding less privileged, Dyson urges." The University Record. January 22, 2001. http://www.ur.umich.edu/0001/Jan22_01/5.htm

hinders the ability to this group to mobilize around group goals.[8] The forces of materialism and individualism can be so strong as to create a myriad of other problems. These are not problems, however, that cannot be overcome. Individualism and materialism can be overcome and dreams can be come reality.

Norton talks about how he was able to gain support in making his dream a reality and then assist others in doing the same,

> **Alexander Norton:** I can recall a time when I went to the bank and I tried to get a Small Business Administration (SBA) loan. I paid a guy $800 to help me with the application.
>
> I was worth over $850,000 at the time. I wanted to borrow $150,000. By this time I had a business, 16 lots, and a house that were all paid for. They wanted me to put all of that up and I turned the check down. My accountant later asked me how I made out with the loan. I told him that I turned it down.
>
> I had to make sure that I wasn't being taken advantage of by anyone. My accountant told me never to tell anyone that I only had a fifth grade education.
>
> I had to learn a lot of things. Most of all I had to learn the system. When I learned the system and I was able to help others. I learned more about financing homes and running my own business.
>
> I was able to use what I learned to help people. I helped people set up businesses. I helped people get Federal Housing Administration (FHA) and veteran loans. I even helped people with bad credit get loans, cause I learned the system.
>
> Before I left Long Island, I could get on the phone and get a quarter of a million dollars from the bank and then come in the morning and sign the check.

[8] See "The Strategic Policies of Affirmative Action," by Peter Skerry. Brookings Institute. http://www.brookings.edu/gs/Skerry_aa.pdf.

Much has been written about the declining or the continuing significance of race. William Julius Wilson and others contend that race has declined in significance rather class determines the life chances of blacks in America. Still others like Joe Feagin contend that race continues to determine life chances for blacks regarding of social class. Norton's experiences on Long Island as an individuals who was increasingly becoming not only economically secure but economically empowered, provides support for the continuing significance of race.

While Norton was learning how to navigate the lending process he was learning that some things on Long Island and in the society at large, had not changed. While he was gaining greater access to financial institutions, he continued to face prejudice and discrimination from the individuals he lived and worked around.

Norton states,

Alexander Norton: Some people on Long Island were very prejudice. Money made it change, though. If you were a wealthy man then the bank doors would be opened to you. The door used to be shut to blacks just because of their race.

Long Island is a rich area. Some people come to the island from New York City and they are not used to having anything. They get a house and they think they are God! They look down on other human beings.

I remember one time I went to the front door, ready to start a job. When I got there the homeowner said, "Boy, the job is at the back and not at the front of the house!"

I said, "There is no boy here. You have to get someone else to do the job!"

Even then, I never got an attitude. I always wanted my customer to be satisfied. I just wanted to get paid and I wanted my customers to tell others about me.

The New York Times is just one news outlet to discuss the issue of prejudice and discrimination on Long Island, especially in the area of housing. In a 1980 article, written during the time that Black Bros Building Corp was operating on Long Island, a journalist by the name of Shawn Kennedy wondered if housing issues there were more a matter of pride or prejudice.[9] He describes Nassau and Suffolk counties as the site of conflicts between two fractions. The first group includes individuals and organizations charged with meeting fair housing and mobility benchmarks, the other includes citizens and local elected officials determined to control their only communities despite federal mandates. Still others think the issues were not really about home rule rather the issues surrounded the exclusion of groups that did not have the characteristics commonly associated with the suburban middle class that dominants the island including the poor and nonwhites.

Race relations are often tense on the island even today. Despite having to overcome barriers to financial, social, and human capital, Al Norton ran a successful business. He defied the odds and secured his share of government contracts. He faced prejudice and discrimination on the individual, community, and institutional levels. He learned the system and did not buck against it. Norton would learn many other lessons. He had learned that hard work paid off, the merits of working hard for your money. Next he would learn how to make his money work for him.

[9] Kennedy, Shawn. June 1, 1980. Is housing on Long Island a matter of pride or prejudice? New York Times. Section 4; Page 6, Column 2; Week in Review Desk.

CHAPTER 5

MAKING YOUR MONEY WORK FOR YOU

Millions of Americans work very hard for their money each day while simultaneously longing for the day when their money will work for them. The question, for many remains, how does one go about making the desire for wealth a reality? How does one become rich rather wealthy if your surname is not Winfrey, Jordan, Buffet, Carnegie, Rockefeller, or Gates? For a time Norton was himself a "Doubting Thomas," unsure how even he with a growing business and experience with rental property, could take the economic status of his company, family, even his community to another level. For Norton, stock ownership was the missing link.

For a time, Norton was like most Americans with an economic portfolio that lacked the diversification that financial experts think everyone should have, rather most Americans have their primary home as the largest, if not the only asset in their portfolio. Still others do not even own their own homes and are drowning in debt. Differences in overall net worth are as American as apple pie. At the root of the problem is the sometimes, gray area between income and wealth.

Some believe that they are rich simply because they have good paying jobs, but income does not equal wealth. This message is critical for people to understand, especially minorities who may not have access to asset owners in their families or even in their neighborhoods. The need to build wealth rather than relying sole on income is a message that Norton hopes to get out especially to young people.

What are the possible relationships between the two concepts and how do these relationships relate to racial and ethnic inequality, especially in the case of black-white differences and differences within the black population?

People that are both income and asset poor are people that have no income and no assets. These people represent individuals and families that are among the most disadvantaged in society in that they have few if any legitimate resources to meet their basic needs and they have no safety net to protect them in the time of economic turbulence. Certain undocumented immigrants and the chronically unemployed are examples of the income and asset poor.

People who have some source of legitimate income yet possess no assets are the income rich and asset poor. While these individuals are able to meet their basic needs, they possess no meaningful buffer against trying economic times. The average black household would fall into this category, as would some whites.

Individuals who earn an income and possess some modest forms of assets represent the average white American household. These individuals and families possess varying levels of income that assists them in meeting their basic needs, and they have some forms of asset ownership such as stocks, homes, other real estate, and business assets. These assets can potentially serve as a cushion in the time of an economic crisis, and when the economic climate is good, others may perceive these people as being quite wealthy. However, people that are dependent upon earned income as well as their wealth do not reflect the wealthiest people in America.

The wealthiest people in America, research has shown, do not have their primary place of residence as the largest or only form of asset ownership as is the case in the average American asset owning household. They are impacted by economic downturns however the extent of their wealth often times leaves them still well above all of the other types of people discussed here. These individuals are not as dependent upon their earned income as others.

Prior research indicates that wealth serves as a buffer for individuals and groups in the time of economic crisis. What do sociologists and scholars from other disciplines have to say about why wealth matters? In the early 1840s de Tocqueville observed that our actions and behaviors as Americans were motivated largely by our desire to accumulate wealth. Additionally, wealth has intergenerational effects in that wealth transfers or inheritance contribute to the quality of education, economic and social opportunities of subsequent generations. Moreover, it has been shown that wealth can contribute to community and economic development. Wealth brings both power and autonomy.

Wealth inequality has grown tremendously since the mid-1960s, perhaps more than originally predicted. Lisa Keister of Wealth Inequality in America found that he mean net worth increased steadily between 1962 and 1989. By the early 1990s, the mean net worth decreased. Overall, Keister found that net worth increased between 1962 and 2000 by more than 50%. There was a steady increase until the mid-1990s and then a downturn in mean average net worth. Keister and others have demonstrated that racial and ethnic differences exist and persist on virtually every wealth category. Racial and ethnic minorities have in many cases not taken part in the wealth boom occurring over

86

the past few decades.

Racial and ethnic differences are perhaps greatest with regards to interest, dividend and rental income. In 1995, over 70% of white households had interest earning assets at financial institutions compared to only less than half of black households. White households had other interest-earning assets more often than black household, according to the U.S. Census.

The racial and ethnic gap concerning stocks and mutual fund shares is also quite wide. Over twenty percent of white households owned stocks and mutual fund shares compared to only five percent of black households. Data from the U.S. Census Bureau also indicate that white households have historically been more likely to own rental property compared to other groups. The percentage of white households who owned rental property according to this report was double the number of black households owned rental property. The percentage of white households who also owned savings bonds were doubled the percentage for black households.

Additionally, about half of all black householders, had a household net worth of less than $10,000 compared to about one-quarter of white householders. For example, black householders are more likely to have a negative net worth when compared to white householders. Twenty-one percent of white households, on the other hand, have a net worth between $100,000 and $249,999 compared to only five percent of blacks, find Oliver and Shapiro, authors of Black Wealth/White Wealth.

Blacks have experienced great discrimination in general and as it relates to wealth. Virtually every racial and minority group in America has experienced past discrimination in terms of education, income, occupation and wealth accumulation. However, studies about wealth inequality demonstrate that racial and ethnic groups have not been and are not equally disadvantaged. So how does one explain racial and ethnic differences in wealth levels and wealth accumulation especially differences in savings and stock ownership? Why have some groups overcome despite the adversity they have historically faced, while others have not? The explanations are diverse and include the following explanations the role of financial inheritance.

Studies have shown that blacks are less likely to possess wealth than their white counterparts at every age and as such are less likely to either give or receive intergenerational transfers of wealth. Not only are whites more likely than nonwhites to receive intergenerational transfers of wealth, but when wealth transfers are made, whites also receive significantly larger amounts than the nonwhites who receive inheritances. Wealth transfers may be used in a variety of ways including college tuition or purchasing a home. We will see later in this book how Al Norton accomplishes this for his children.

Keister observes that inheritance produces and perpetuates wealth inequality but argues that the degree to which individuals and families have been able to transfer wealth has changed over time. Keister also notes that in the 19th century wealth was achieved through land ownership when land was made available in bulk from the federal government to homesteaders. Moreover, it is noted that many working-class Americans experienced upward social mobility by way of cheap housing prices, expanded educational opportunities and over all growth in the economy. Clearly, whites were able to benefit from these opportunities for massive wealth accumulation, while nonwhites were limited in their ability to capitalize on these historic moments based not solely on their credit worthiness but by another inherited characteristic, their race. The mere presence of black households and other racial and ethnic minority household was a signal to potential investors, mortgage lenders and consumers of the quality of investment. Such practices were promoted by government agencies and later adapted by other financial institutions.

Moreover it is noted that with inheritance comes political power, social contacts and economic advantage. Each link enables the wealthy to transfer assets from one generation to the next. The wealthy use their political and economic advantages to ensure that government policies will facilitate the transfer of wealth from generation to generation and not impede that process. The implication is that wealth inequality, as a form of racial and ethnic inequality, is maintained if not worsened.

Investing can lead to economic empowerment for many. Alexander Norton went from having being among the many Americans with little or no interest, dividends and rental income to being among those with significant levels. The following tables, labeled 1 through 10, show just how different levels of interest, dividends and rental income are for most. The tables were created using census data collected over the past several decades.

Al Norton became familiar with investing through a long-term relationship he developed with a banker.

> **Alexander Norton:** I had been doing business with this one bank for nineteen years. The guy I was dealing with told me that he was going to retire. He says to me, "Why don't you invest? You can make a lot more money."
>
> I replied, "What do you mean? Why didn't you tell me years ago?"

He said that he would call headquarters and give me some more information.

My wife and I returned to the bank. When we got there, he started telling us where we could put money to make money. He told me that the more money you have the more you can make. He introduced me to tax shelters. He said invest $100,000 in a tax shelter and you won't have to pay a dime in taxes. In the next few years you will have $200,000.

I smiled and I said tell me something else. He said that it was the truth.

Jeff Schnepper of MSNBC defines tax shelters as an investment designed to avoid or to reduce income taxes. Conventional tax shelters have included oil, gas, real estate, equipment leasing, even cattle feeding and breeding programs says Schnepper. Tax shelters when introduced were very controversial. Leonard Burman, an affiliate of the Urban Institute, expressed some of the key issues associated with this controversy in a 2006 article entitled, "The Tax Reform Act of 2010." He says, twenty years ago tax reforms aimed at closing he loopholes associated with tax shelters were introduced. Prior to reform measures, "rich people could engineer transactions to avoid all or most of their tax liability. Voters believed the tax system was unfair and cheating was thought to be on the rise. Those problems exist to some extent today."

Alexander Norton: I was on a job one time. I was doing work for a Mr. Martin in Amityville. He told me that he used to put groceries on the shelf before he made his money in the stock market and he did very well. That was the reason that I got involved with stocks. I didn't know anything about it when I started but I learned.

I went out and brought 2,500 shares each for me, my wife, and sons. I told them to watch the stock. I believe that you can learn by doing. I was business running my business and they were busy going to school but I told each of them to watch their shares.

Within six months the stocks when from $13.58 share to $32.50. I decided that I was going to sell. I tell you, I made more money in one year in the stock market than on my business.

I got into the stock market when Regan came out with a goodie! We were putting money in there for retirement. Regan came out with a plan where what you made in dividends you could invest it back and get double!

I told my accountant that I was going to take my money out of my 401. I told him that I did not want the government investing my money. I believed that I could invest my own money. Within six months I was making money. I told him that I was not worried about Social Security. I was more interested in long-term investing. I knew that investments could give me more than the government would ever pay.

I made a lot of money and I tried to share what I learned with others. Some listened and others did not. Some people hear but they don't hear. It goes in one ear and out the other with some people.

I told this one guy about investing. He became a teacher but he started out as a painter. I talked to him about the many mistakes that I saw people make. One of the biggest mistakes that people make is that they start doing good and they immediately start living good.

I told him, like I tell other people. You can't have a half a cup of water and think that you can drink forever. Some people get money in their pockets and they buy boats and cars. I told him to watching his spending. Invest for a few years. Put the money that you plan to invest in a separate account, like in a six year account. Invest in a tax shelter or insurance company where they pay you more than the bank. Most people just don't know about these opportunities to growing wealth.

There is plenty of money out there if we can only open our ears and listen; if we can only open our eyes and look for it. Investing is really something that you have to do for yourself. No one is going to do it for you.

We have to do a better job of saving. So what if you look pretty and you are driving a nice car, but just driving a nice car is not getting it! Stocks are a good thing to play with.

Just get started. We have to learn some way.

If I could do it all over again, I would do the same exact thing, because it works.

Real estate is another good investment so are mutual funds. Any young person can make it with investments, they don't know because no one has taught them. Many young people borrow $20,000 for a car when they could take that same money and invest it instead and once a person reaches that $100,000, the ladder starts to come to you.

The economic policies of the Regan administration played an important role in the wealth accumulation process for Alexander Norton as it did for many others. Regan's economic policies have received praise from some and critiques by others. Scholars have written about the administration and federalism, deficits, education fiscal policy, food assistance programs, South Africa, and human rights. An article entitled, "Regan's Economic Policies: A Critique," which appeared in an edition of Oxford Economic Papers in 1988 addresses some of the issues that the nation was facing at the time and how Regan addressed each.

In the decades leading up to Regan's victory, the nation experienced record levels of unemployment, inflation and two oil crises. High budget deficits existed in 1977, 1978 and 1980. Regan likened the situation to the Great Depression, although some disagreed with the comparison. He blamed runaway deficits, increase in the national debt, increases in the percent of earnings the government took in taxes between 1960 and 1980 for much of the nation's problems. High inflation, increases in mortgage rates over time, and seven million unemployed Americans were evidenced of the economic crisis Regan sought to address.

In the end, the nation experienced the myriad of problems outlined above because of failed government policies. Government expenditures grew out of control. Relaxing government spending and reducing personal income tax rates were among the solutions proposed by Regan, some contend at great social costs.

The Kemp-Roth Act of August 1981, the introduction of IRAs and Tax Reform Acts of 1986 are among the actions taken under the Regan administration aimed at reducing inflation, increasing savings and investments, and decreasing government expenditures that hurt some but helped Norton. Norton was impacted by some of the negative social costs associated with Reganomics as well as a number of policies from subsequent administrations. The following table provides a cross-sectional view of overall net worth during for households during the Regan administration based upon race and Hispanic origin.

Median Net Worth, by Race and Spanish Origin of Householder and
Monthly Household Income: 1984

Monthly household income	Total	White	Black	Spanish origin[1]
All households......................(thousands)..	86,790	75,343	9,509	4,162
Median income	$ 1,677	$ 1,760	$ 1,088	$ 1,345
Median net worth	32,667	39,135	3,397	4,913
Net Worth by Income				
Less than $900:				
Households ....(thousands)..	22,297	17,753	4,081	1,345
Median net worth	$ 5,080	$ 8,443	$ 88	$ 453
$900 to $1,999:				
Households ....(thousands)..	26,599	23,021	3,004	1,447
Median net worth	$ 24,647	$ 30,714	$ 4,218	$ 3,677
$2,000 to $3,999:				
Households ....(thousands)..	27,173	24,573	2,009	1,105
Median net worth	$46,744	$50,529	$15,977	$24,805
$4,000 or more:				
Households ....(thousands)..	10,720	9,995	416	265
Median net worth	$123,474	$128,237	$58,758	$99,492
Type of Household				
Married-couple households:				
Number.........................(thousands)..	50,606	45,873	3,507	2,443
Median net worth	$50,116	$54,184	$13,061	$10,823
Female householders:				
Number.........................(thousands)..	23,596	18,831	4,392	1,125
Median net worth	$13,885	$22,500	$ 671	$ 478
Male householders:				
Number.........................(thousands)..	12,588	10,639	1,611	593
Median net worth	$9,883	$11,826	$3,022	$2,703

[1]Persons of Spanish origin may be of any race.

While Al Norton's socioeconomic status was improving, while he was moving further towards economic empowerment, many others in Coram were chronically economically insecure. Changes on Long Island, forced Norton out.

> **Alexander Norton:** I had one of the finest houses but I had to walk with a gun. I helped the community and still these young punks tried to rob me! I really liked it on Long Island. I educated my children here but my children encouraged me to leave, they said, "Daddy, you should not have to live like this!"

Drugs and violence were contributing to the overcrowding of jails in Nassau and Suffolk counties during the 1980s. The trend continued in the 1990s and led Norton to move his family to a rural community in upstate New York, a community where he would again construct his own home, brick by brick, little by little, on the weekends, on nearly 100 acres of coveted real estate. New Berlin would also be the site of one of the

Norton family's worse personal tragedies, a fatal accident that took the life of his beloved

wife, Alcesta.

CHAPTER 6

MOVING ON AND PAYING IT FORWARD

New Berlin is a far cry from what comes to mind for most people when they think of New York. New Berlin is a small village in upstate New York about an hours drive to Utica. Yet it is home to many residents, formerly of Suffolk County, including many retired police officers. Even in a place like New Berlin, Norton runs into people who grew up in Long Island and remember him from his days as the owner of Black Bro Building Corp.

Norton was ready at the age of 58 to retire from the construction industry and build the home that he and his wife dreamed of building in the country. The two dreamed of a home that would sit in the middle of 100 acres. Unable to convince even one of his three sons to take on the business, Norton sold Black Bro Building Corp and headed for greener pastures.

New Berlin, while home to many former residents of Long Island, is very different. A demographic analysis of the two areas further illustrates the sharp contrasts. The population of Coram is substantially larger than New Berlin. Almost 35,000 people call Coram home while only 1,129 people live in New Berlin. About 82% of the residents of Coram are white compared to 98% of the residents in New Berlin. Almost 10% of Coram's population is black and about 3% are Asian. Hispanics, who can be of any race, make up about 10% of Coram's population. Less than 1% of New Berlin's population was black. Asians made up 0.3% of residents in New Berlin while Hispanics made up 0.9%. Clearly, New Berlin is less diverse racially and ethnically than Coram.

Residents in Coram and in New Berlin are more likely to be homeowners than renters. In Coram, 69% of residents own their own homes compared to 62% in New Berlin. About 31% of Coram residents rent while 38% of residents in New Berlin rent. Coram residents not only have higher percentages of home ownership but they also have higher percentages of people with four-year degrees. Twenty-six percent of people living in Coram reported during the last decennial census that they earned at least a Bachelor's Degree while only 17% of New Berlin respondents said the same.

Nor only are Coram residents more educated formerly, they also have higher percentages of labor force participate. In Coram, 70% of residents are in the labor force compared to just over half of people living in New Berlin. It is no wonder then why differences in the poverty levels were observed too. Six percent of individuals in Coram reported living in poverty compared to almost 20% of individuals in New Berlin. Coram residents earned more than twice what residents in New Berlin earned. On average, household income in Coram is $61,309 while average household income in New Berlin is $27,885.

Coram residents have higher levels of income and education when compared with their neighbors to the North. Greater access to human capital as well as differences in the real estate market, allow people living in Coram to purchase homes that are worth significantly more than the average home in New Berlin. The average home in Coram, New York, is worth about $158,000 while the average home in New Berlin is worth about a third of that, $53,400.

Despite the social and demographic differences between New Berlin and Coram, Norton was happy with the choice that he made with his wife to move. Norton and his wife made themselves at home in the community. Both were active participants in their local church and in the local political scene. The connectedness of this couple to the community was particularly evident when Alexander Norton's wife, Alcesta Norton, was killed in a car accident in April 1999. A busload came from Coram to be with Norton and his family. The town even named a park in honor of Alcesta. Her legacy lives on couple's three children.

Al and Alcesta were able to pay for their three children's education. Alexander, Stanley, and Theodore (Teddy), all graduated from college, gained experience in the stock market and in other financial areas. Stanley and Teddy entered into the field of technology. Stanley currently works as an administrator in a hospital in New Jersey. Al Norton helped Teddy establish a business in Boston, Massachusetts where he sells and repairs personal computers. Alexander Norton, Jr. joined the military and ultimately became a physician. He has taken an interest in real estate has well.

> **Alexander Norton**: My son lives in Nevada. He brought his first house and then he sold it at a profit of $53,000. He put $50,000 into a CD. He went to Tokyo for two years and when he returned he brought a house for $350,000. Within 3 years he sold that house for $750,000. Next house he built cost him a million dollars and he sold that one and made $2.5 million. He invests. He is a doctor and he makes over a million dollars a year. In fact, he just brought a building for $7.5 million for his practice, which a number of doctors share.

Norton would like to see other young people enjoy the success that his own sons experienced. His goal is to share what he has learned with others. He was able to do so with Lucy Merriweather his now wife. She had no experience with the stock market before meeting Al Norton and has since that time done quite well. While Norton may have faced barriers to financial, human and social capital himself, once he became economically empowered, he was able to assist remove some of these barriers for those around him. His life story is an excellent case study of one man's voyage from poverty to prosperity and his effort to lift others along the way. It provides insight about the pathway to asset ownership.

Since Al Norton started his business in the early 1970s, much has changed especially racial and ethnic differences. While homeownership increased for each racial and ethnic group over time that racial and ethnic gaps persisted including between blacks and whites. Over time whites consistently were twice as likely to be homeowners than their black counterparts. The results also indicted that while homeownership increased and while the racial and ethnic gap in ownership was about the same, the racial and ethnic gap in housing values between blacks and whites has grown over time even after controlling for selected social and demographic variables.

Additionally, a narrowing of the gap with regards to the relative odds of business ownership between racial groups was observed. An analysis conducted by the author finds that whites in 1970 were 3.38 times more likely to own a business than blacks during the same year but only 2.76 times more likely in 2000. Racial and ethnic differences on business income also persisted but were relatively unchanged over time. The greatest difference between whites and non-whites was found on the likelihood of owning interest, dividends and rental income. Whites, for example, were more than 5 times more likely to have interest, dividends and rental income when compared to blacks and Hispanics and more than twice as likely to have this form of asset ownership relative to other respondents. The differences in the likelihood of having interest, dividends and rental income were somewhat higher in the earlier decades. Additionally, the findings showed that the gap between whites and non-whites increased with regards to interest, dividends and rental income over time. Total income from assets has increased for all racial and ethnic groups between 1980 and 2000 although whites consistently had higher absolute levels of income from assets. Whites also tended to have higher percentages of income from assets even when income was considered. Whites with lower earning levels had substantially higher percentages of income from assets than higher earnings while the percentage of income from assets for black respondents was about the same regardless of income levels.

For black ethnic groups the findings revealed that the likelihood of owing a home over time after controlling for a series of social and demographic factors that Afro-Caribbean respondents had the highest odds of homeownership followed by African-Americans and Africans. African-Americans reported relatively higher housing values in 1980 but had housing values that were lower than Afro-Caribbean subjects in later decades and higher housing values than Africans during the same time period.

The significance of black ethnicity on the likelihood of business ownership increased over time. Black ethnicity was not a significant determinant of business ownership in 1980 but was a significant determinant by 2000. Black ethnicity, however, was not a significant determinant of business income in 1980 or in 2000. Afro-Caribbean and African subjects had higher percentages of business ownership than for selected social and demographic variables. After controlling for these variables African-Americans were slightly more likely than Afro-Caribbean subjects to be business owners in 2000 but not significantly different from Africans. Afro-Caribbean subjects the most advantaged black ethnic group a decade earlier with no difference among groups in 1980.

Moreover, the findings revealed that in each decade that African-Americans had the lowest likelihood of interest, dividend and rental property ownership although the odds of having this dependent variable have increased over time. The gap between black ethnic groups on interest, dividends and rental income increased over time between Afro-Caribbean and African-American subjects while no differences were observed between African-Americans and Africans. The findings concerning total income from assets and percentage of income from assets for black ethnic groups were consistent with the patterns observed for blacks as observed in the analyses, which included blacks regardless of their ethnicity.

For each dependent variable, during each decade considered, the results showed that blacks lagged behind whites and other minority groups. Even after adding the selected social and demographic variables racial and ethnic differences in the likelihood of business ownership and homeownership as well as on the predicted levels of housing values, business income, income and interest, dividends and rental income, persisted. These observations support race-based theories that argue that race continues to be significant in determining the life chances of all Americans, for some it brings about various privileges, for others their racial identification comes at great cost. Racial formation asserts this as well.

Some contend that race has been and continues to shape both identities and institutions in significant ways and the same could be said for ethnicity, to a lesser degree.   Understanding the causes and consequences of intergroup relations allows researchers to enhance our ability to observe how race and racism change over time. Some argue that race is most commonly conceptualized as a fixed concept or as a fictitious attribute that a color-blind new social order would eradicate. Despite a lack of agreement about what race is and what it is not, the most important factor to note is that race continues to play an important role in structuring and representing our view of the world in general and our view of American society in particular.

Whites had the highest housing values, business incomes, incomes and interest dividends and rental income and blacks had the lowest between 1970 and 2000. Whites were also more likely than blacks to own a home and to own a business between 1970 and 2000. The findings also showed that respondents of Afro-Caribbean descent had the higher housing values, interests, dividends and rental income, and incomes than other blacks between 1980 and 2000. African respondents, however, had the highest business incomes among the black ethnic groups, with African-Americans have the lowest levels over time.

However, the finding that racial differences decreased when selected control variables were added shows that variations in homeownership, housing values, business ownership, business income, income and interest, dividends and rental income between blacks and whites can be explained by factors other than race including indicators such as education and occupational score.   These findings support class-based perspectives including several introduced by William Julius Wilson. Wilson linked arguments about race to changes in economic structure, which ultimately led to the conclusion that class is more of a determinant of life chances, particularly for blacks in America, than is race. He argues that there have been structural and economical shifts occurring during the pre-industrial, industrial and post-industrial periods, which have coincided with changes in race relations which contributed to an absence of a uniform black experience based on race. Instead, blacks experienced America in profoundly different ways.

Wilson claims that race has often been used to exploit underlying economic goals. Wilson notes that in American history black workers were often used as pawns in labor disputes between business owners and white workers. Blacks were used as strikebreakers, for example. He contends that the business class used race to take attention away from class domination repeatedly whether it was on the plantation or in the factory. He further adds that class conflict between white labor and management produced racial conflict between blacks and whites.

Nonetheless, Wilson believes that the major support for what he calls the declining significance of race thesis is evidenced by the expansion of the middle-class and the growth and increasing concentration of the bottom or underclass. In the Truly Disadvantaged, Wilson furthers his argument about the supremacy of economic position in the lives of blacks in America. He directly attributes the presence of such problems as violent crimes, out-of-wedlock births, female-headed families and welfare-dependency to the increasing social dislocation of a distinct disadvantaged class of blacks in America. Again, he attributes this disadvantaged position, not to race or racism, but to changes in the urban economy, joblessness and class transformation. The underclass, according to Wilson, was established as a result of racial discrimination in the past, social policies that targeted the already advantaged and the economic restructuring of the American economy, including deindustrialization. Variations in the types and levels of assets owned between blacks and whites and within the black population provide support for Wilson's arguments. Additionally, the findings that racial and ethnic differences are diminished when control variables are included also provide support for Wilson's views. Factors other than race and ethnicity clearly help to explain variations on indicators of asset ownership. Individuals regardless of race and ethnicity benefited from their investments into education and with regards to occupational score, two indicators of socioeconomic status although to varying degrees. Blacks with relatively high levels of education and occupational score fared better consistently than other blacks.

Partial support for assimilation theories was also evident. Assimilation theory addresses several other key issues. Two themes have dominated the literature on race and ethnicity and spatial processes, assimilation and spatial assimilation (Logan, Alba and Leung 1996). Early theorists argued that minority groups, including new arrivals to the United States would eventually undergo a process by which they would be incorporated into mainstream American society. However, this classical description of the assimilation process ignored spatial processes (Massey and Mullan 1984). Empirical tests of these theories have shown that this is not always the case.

Massey and Mullan (1984) found that blacks, regardless of their nativity, face strong barriers to spatial assimilation, which causes them to be isolated spatially from whites. The authors also found that disadvantage follows upwardly mobile blacks as they attempt to assimilate spatially. Moreover, assimilation theory suggests that as length of residency increases that the likelihood of asset ownership and the levels of incomes and values of assets should increase. It also suggests that respondents that speak only English should be more likely to own homes and businesses than their bilingual counterparts and that they should have higher housing values, business incomes, incomes and interest, dividends and rental income. Assimilation theory also implies that foreign-born blacks should have lower levels of asset ownership and lower values on each asset. The findings somewhat contradict assimilation in important ways especially in the better position of Afro-Caribbean subjects. Additionally, foreign-born blacks consistently did better than their native-born counterparts.

In 2000 for example, bilingualism was clearly a disadvantage in the general model with regards to homeownership, newer arrivals had lower odds of homeownership than older arrivals, and the foreign-born had higher odds of homeownership. The same general patterns were observed for housing values although respondents proficient in English had relatively higher housing values than respondents that spoke only English. Concerning business ownership, bilingualism was clearly an advantage in the general model while the patterns for year of immigration and nativity were consistent with those observed on home ownership and housing values. Conversely for business income not only was bilingualism not universally advantageous but business income was actually higher for newer arrivals than for older arrivals and the foreign-born reported relatively lower levels of business income than their native-born counterparts. These patterns were consistent for black except that the foreign-born were consistently more advantaged than the native-born. Bilingual respondents were at a clear disadvantage with regards to the likelihood of having interest, dividends and rental income and on the levels of interest, dividends and rental income when compared with respondents that spoke only English while older arrivals and those that were foreign-born were advantaged. English proficient was not a significant predictor of interest, dividends and rental income in the model for blacks. Assimilation may be more advantageous on certain types of assets than on other assets and assimilation may be more advantageous for some racial and ethnic groups than for others.

Clearly, no one perspective explains racial and ethnic differences on homeownership, housing values, business ownership, business income, income or interest, dividends and rental income. Support, at least in part, for race-based, class-based and assimilation theories were found. Neither perspective fully accounts for the persistence of racial differences on the dependent variables taken together they demonstrate the complex pathways and asset ownership both black and white respondents.

Greater attention must be given to racial and ethnic inequality in wealth and the roles of residential segregation, inheritance, occupational-based stock ownership, and social policies. Perhaps the continued residential segregation of Americans, particularly blacks and whites, may explain the increase in racial inequality on housing values while homeownership has grown.   Many blacks continue to live in hypersegregated communities where housing values may be lower due in part to the concentration and/or absence of a given racial or ethnic group. This hypersegregation of racial and ethnic groups may be due to prejudice, perceived social class differences or mere in-group preferences (Bobo 1996).

The gap between blacks and whites was notable on interest, dividends, and rental income and increased over time. This observation may be explained by variations in social capital, human capital and savings/consumption patterns. Since racial and ethnic minorities have relatively low levels of income when compared with whites they may have less to save and thus enjoy lower interest levels. Racial and ethnic differences in the transfer of wealth through inheritance may also explain differences on interest levels. Since whites inherit more than nonwhites they may be able to place some of the monetary inheritance into an interest bearing account. The inheritance could be in the form of a second home which may be used to generate rental income which might account for racial differences on this indicator as well.

Since blacks have relatively lower levels of income they may be less willing to endure the risks associated with investment in the stock market and as such have lower dividend levels. Racial and ethnic minorities may also be in occupations where stock ownership is not part of any benefit package or pension plan which may also account for the racial and ethnic differences. These differences have likely grown over time which in turn may have contributed to persistent racial and ethnic differences on interest, dividends and rental income.

Few social and public policies have been created specifically for the purpose of increasing interest, dividends and rental income. Most policies have focused on the promotion of homeownership and on the promotion of minority-business ownership which has grown over time. While ownership has increased, the return on investment is not as great for racial and ethnic minorities as it for the dominant group. Perhaps future policies should focus not only on increasing the types of assets owned but on increasing the levels of assets owned.

Alexander Norton's life story serves as an interesting case study. His story shows one man's journey from economic insecurity to business owner to philanthropists. With just a fifth grade education, he took his hands out of the dishwater and into the market. He is proof positive of just how far some disadvantaged groups have come, particularly blacks who began life in America as assets and many are now owners. Most research about the role to wealth tends to focus on the Warren Buffets of the world. Additional attention should be devoted to understanding the pathway to asset ownership for members of historically disadvantaged groups in an effort to set more on the pathway from economic insecurity to economic empowerment.

Bibliography and Suggestions for Further Readings on Race and Wealth

Adelman, Robert, Chris Morett and Stewart Tolnay. 2000. Homeward Bound: The Return Migration of Southern-Born Black Women, 1940-1990. *Sociological Spectrum.* 20(4): 433-463.

Alba, Richard. 1990. Ethnic Identities. CT: Yale University Press.

Alba, Richard and John R. Logan. 1991. Variations on Two Themes: Racial and Ethnic Patterns in the Attainment of Suburban Residence. *Demography*, Vol. 28(3):431-453.

Alba, Richard and John R. Logan. 1992. Assimilation and Stratification in the Homeownership Patterns of Racial and Ethnic Groups. *International Migration Review*, Vol. 26(4):1314-1341.

Alba, Richard and Victor Nee. 1997. "Rethinking assimilation theory for a new era of immigration," *International Migration Review* 31: 826-74.

Alba, Richard, John Logan, Brian Stults and Gilbert Marzan and Wenquan Zhang. 1999. Immigrant Groups and Suburbs: A Reexamination of Suburbanization and Spatial Assimilation. *American Sociological Review.* 64: 446-60.

Allen, Beverlyn Lundy. 2002. Race and Gender Inequality in Homeownership: Does Place Matter. *Rural Sociology. 67:* 603-621.

Alston, Lee and Joseph Ferrie. 1985. Labor Costs, Paternalism, and Loyalty in Southern Agriculture. *Journal of Economic History.* 45:95-117.

Andersen, Margaret and Patricia Hill Collins. 2001. *Race, Class and Gender.* CA: Wadsworth.

Anderson, Margo and Stephen Fienberg. 1999. *Who Counts? The Politics of Census-Taking in Contemporary America.* NY: Russell Sage Foundation.

Astone, Nan Marie, Constance Nathanson, Robert Schoen and Young Kim. 1999. Family Demography, Social Theory, and Investment in Social Capital. *Population and Development Review* 25(1): 1-31.

Attanasio, Orazio and Hilary Williamson. 2000. Differential Mortality and Wealth Accumulation. *The Journal of Human Resources.* 35(1): 1-29.

Avery, Robert and Michael Rendall. 2002. Lifetime Inheritances of Three Generations of Whites and Blacks. American Journal of Sociology. 107:1300-1346.

Barnett, Bernice McNair. 1993. Invisible Southern Black Women Leaders in the Civil Rights Movement: The Triple Constraints of Gender, Race, and Class. *Gender and Society,* Vol. 7(2): 162-182.

Bean, Frank and Stephanie Bell-Rose. 1999. *Immigration and Opportunity.* NY: Russell Sage.

Beckles, Hilary. 1997. Capitalism, Slavery and Caribbean Modernity. *Callaloo.* 20(4): 777-789.

Berlin, Ira. 1974. *Slaves Without Masters.* NY: Oxford University Press.

Bielby, William and Denise Bielby. 1999. Organizational Mediation of Project-Based Labor Markets: Talent Agencies and the Careers of Screenwriters. *American Sociological Review.* 64(1): 64-85.

Billingsley, Andrew. 1992. *Climbing Jacob's Ladder: The Enduring Legacy of African-American Families.* Touchstone: NY.

Blackwell, James. 1991. *The Black Community.* NY: Harper and Row.

Blalock, Herbert. 1967. *Towards a Theory of Minority-Group Relations.* NY: Capricorn Books.

Blauner, Robert. 1972. Racial oppression in America. NY: Harper and Row.

Bloeman, Hans and Stancanelli, Elena. 2001. Individual Wealth, Reservation Wages and Transitions into Employment. Journal of Labor Economics. 19(2):400-439.

Bloom, Jack. 1987. *Class, Race, and the Civil Rights Movement*. Indiana: Indiana University Press.

Boahen, Adu. 1999. *Topics in West African History*. Pearson Education.

Bobo, Lawrence and Camille Zubrinsky. 1996. Attitudes on Residential Integration: Perceived Status Differences, Mere In-Group Preference, or Racial Prejudice? *Social Forces*, Vol. 74(3):883-909.

Bobo, Lawrence, Melvin Oliver, James Johnson and Abel Valenzuela. 2000. *Prismatic Metropolis*. NY: Russell Sage Foundation.

Bodenhorn, Howard. 2002. The Complexion Gap: The Economic Consequences of Color among Free African Americans in the Rural Antebellum South. *National Bureau of Economic Research Working Paper No. w8957.*

Bonacich, Edna. 1976. Advanced Capitalism and Black/White Race Relations in the United States: A Split Labor Market Interpretation. *American Sociological Review*. 41(1): 34-51.

Bonacich, Edna. 1975. Abolition, the Extension of Slavery, and the Position of Free Blacks: A Study of Split Labor Markets in the United States, 1830-1863. *American Journal of Sociology*. 81(3):601-628.

Bonilla-Silva, Eduardo. 2001. *White Supremacy and Racism in the Post-Civil Rights Era*. CO: Lynne Rienner.

Boyd, Robert. 2000. Race, Labor Market Disadvantage, and Survivalist Entrepreneurship: Black Women in the Urban North during the Great Depression. *Sociological Forum*. 15(4): 647-670.

Brown, Cliff. 2000. The Role of Employers in Split Labor Markets: An Event Structure Analysis of Racial Conflict and AFL Organizing, 1917-1919. *Social Forces*. 79(2): 653-681.

Bryce-Laporte, Roy Simon. 1972. Black Immigrants. *Journal of Black Studies*. 3(1): 29-56.

Butcher, Kristin. 1994. Black Immigrants in the United States. *Industrial and Labor Relations Review*. 47(2): 265-284.

Butler, John S. 1991. *Entrepreneurship and Self-help among Black Americans*. NY:State University of New York Press.

Butler, John S. 2001. Comments. In *Assets for the Poor*. Shapiro, Thomas and Wolff, Edward, editors. NY: Russell Sage Foundation.

Cancio, A. Silvia, T. David Evans and David Maume. 1996. Reconsidering the Declining Significance of Race. *American Sociological Review*. 61(4): 541-556.

Cantave, Cassandra and Roderick Harrison. 2001. *Historic Trends I*. The Joint Center for Political and Economic Studies.

Charles, Kerwin Kofi and Erik Hurst. 2002. "The Transition to Home Ownership and the Black White Wealth Gap. Review of Economics and Statistics. 84:281-97.

Chevan, Albert. 1989. The Growth of Home Ownership: 1940-1980. Demography. 26(2):249-266.

Cohen, Philip. 1998. Black Concentration Effects on Black-White and Gender Inequality: Multilevel Analysis for U.S. Metropolitan Areas. *Social Forces*, Vol. 77(1):207-229.

Collins, Patricia Hill. 2000. *Black Feminist Thought*. NY: Routledge.

Collins, William and Robert Margo. 2001. Race and Home Ownership in Twentieth Century America: The Role of Sample Composition. Working Paper. No. 01-W10.

Coleman, James. 1988. Social Capital in the Creation of Human Capital. *American Journal of Sociology*. 94: S95-120.

Conley, D Dalton. 1999. *Being Black, Living in the Red*. Berkeley: University of California Press.

Cotter, David, Joan Hermsen and Reeve Vanneman. 2001. Women's Work and Working Women. *Gender and Society*. 15(3): 429-452.

Crowder, Kyle. 2001. Racial Stratification in the Actuation of Mobility Expectations: Microlevel Impacts of Racially Restrictive Housing Markets. *Social Forces*, Vol. 79 (4):1377-1396.

Dahms, Harry. 1997. Theory in Weberian Marxism. *Sociological Theory*. 15(3): 181-214.

Darden, Joe. 1995. Black Residential Segregation Since the 1948 Shelley V. Kraemer Decision. *Journal of Black Studies*, Vol. 25(6): 680-691.

Davis, Angela. 1983. *Women, Race and Class*. NY: Vintage.

Denton, Nancy. 2001. Housing as a Means of Asset Accumulation. In *Assets for the Poor*. Shapiro, Thomas and Wolff, Edward, editors. 232-268. NY: Russell Sage Foundation.

Derby, Lauren. 1994. Haitians, Magic, and Money. *Comparative Studies in Society and History*. 36(3): 488-526.

Dickens, William T. and Kevin Lang. 1985. "Testing Dual Labor Market Theory: A Reconsideration of the Evidence." Working Paper No.1670, *National Bureau of Economic Research*, Chicago, IL.

Dodoo, F. Nii-Amoo. 1997. Assimilation Differences among Africans in America. *Social Forces*. 76(2): 527-546.

Drake, St. Clair and Horace Cayton. 1945. *Black Metropolis*. NY: Harcourt, Brace and company

Duncan, Otis Dudley. 1961. A Socioeconomic Index for all Occupations. Pp. 108-34 in *Occupations and Social Status*, edited by A. Reiss. New York: Free Press.

Eaton, William and Roberta Garrison. 1992. Mental Health in Mariel Cubans and Haitian Boat People. *International Migration Review*. 26(4): 1395-1415.

Edin, Kathryn. 2001. More than Money. In *Assets for the Poor*. Shapiro, Thomas and Wolff, Edward, editors. 206-231. NY: Russell Sage Foundation.

Eggerling-Boeck, Jennifer. 2002. Issues of Black Identity: A Review of Literature. *African American Research Perspectives*. 8(1):17-26.

Emerson, Michael, Yancey, George and Karen Chai. 2001. Does Race Matter in Residential Segregation? Exploring the Preferences of White Americans. *American Sociological Review*. 66:922-935.

Gibson, Margaret. (1989). *Accommodation without Assimilation: Sikh Immigrants in an American High School*. Ithaca: Cornell University Press.

Goldstein, Joshua and Catherine Kenney. 2001. Marriage Delayed or Marriage Foregone. *American Sociological Review*. 66(4): 506-519.

Grodsky, Eric and Devah Pager. 2001. The Structure of Disadvantage: Individual and Occupational Determinants of the Black-White Wage Gap. *American Sociological Review*. Vol 66(4): 542-567.

Feagin, Joe. (1991). The Continuing Significance of Race. *American Sociological Review*. (56): 101-116.

Feagin, Joe and Hernan Vera. 1995. *White Racism*. NY: Routledge.

Feagin, Joe and Melvin Sikes. 1994. *Living with Racism*. MA: Beacon Press.

Feagin, Joe. 1999. Excluding Blacks and Others From Housing: The Foundation of White Racism. *Cityscape*. Vol. 4. No.3.

Flippen, Chenoa. 2004. Unequal Returns to Housing Investments? A Study of Real Housing Appreciation among Black, White, and Hispanic Households. Social Forces. 82:1523-5.

Gibson, Margaret. (1989). *Accommodation without Assimilation: Sikh Immigrants in an American High School*. Ithaca: Cornell University Press.

Gordon, Milton. 1964. *Assimilation in American Life*. NY: Oxford University Press.

Gossett, Thomas. 1997. *Race: The History of an Idea in America*. NY: Oxford University Press.

Grannis, Rick. 1998. The Importance of Trivial Streets: Residential Streets and Residential Segregation. *American Journal of Sociology*, Vol. 103(6): 1530-1564.

Granovetter, Mark. 1995. The Economic Sociology of Firms and Entrepreneurs. In *The Economic Sociology of Immigrants*. 128-65. Edited by Alejandro Portes. NY: Russell Sage.

Grodsky, Eric and Devah Pager. 2001. The Structure of Disadvantage: Individual and Occupational Determinants of the Black-White Wage Gap. *American Sociological Review*. Vol 66(4): 542-567.

Harker, Kathryn. 2001. Immigrant Generation, Assimilation and Adolescent Psychological Well-Being. *Social Forces*. 79(3):964-1004.

Harrison, Roderick and Claudette Bennett. 1995. Racial and Ethnic Diversity. In *State of the Union*. Edited by Reynolds Farley. Volume Two. 141-210.

Hayward, Mark, Eileen Crimmins, Toni Miles and Yu Yang. 2000. The Significance of Socioeconomic Status in Explaining the Racial Gap in Chronic Health Conditions. *American Sociological Review*. 65:910-930.

Heaton, John and Deborah Lucas. 2000. Portfolio Choice and Asset Price. *Journal of Finance*.

Horton, Hayward Derrick, Melvin Thomas, and Cedric Herring. 1995. Rural-Urban Differences in Black Family Structure: An Analysis of the 1990 Census. *Journal of Family Issues* 16:298-313.

Horton, Hayward Derrick and Melvin Thomas. 1998. Race, Class and Family Structure: Differences in Housing Values for Black and White Homeowners. *Sociological Inquiry*. 68: 114-136.

Horton, Hayward Derrick. 1999. Critical Demography. *Sociological Forum.* 14(3):369-398.

Horton, Hayward Derrick, Beverlyn Lundy Allen, Cedric Herring and Melvin Thomas. 2000. Lost in the Storm. *American Sociological Review.* 65:128-137.

Horton, Hayward Derrick and Lori Latrice Sykes. 2004. Toward a Critical Demography of Neo-Mulattos. In *Skin Deep.* Edited by C. Herring, V. Keith and H.D. Horton.

Hout, Michael. 1984. Occupational Mobility of Black Men. *American Sociological Review.* 49(3): 308-322.

Huie, Stephanie, Patrick Krueger, Richard Rogers, and Robert Hummer. 2003. Wealth, Race and Mortality. Social Science Quarterly. 84:667-84.

Hull, Kathleen and Robert Nelson. 2000. Assimilation, Choice or Constraint. *Social Forces.* 79(1):229-264.

Hunter, Margaret. 2002. If You're Light You're Alright: Light Skin as Social Capital for Women of Color. *Gender and Society.* Vol 16(2): 175-193.

Hwang, Sean-Shong and Steve Murdock. 1998. Racial Attraction or Racial Avoidance in American Suburbs? *Social Forces.* 541-565.

Kalmijn, Matthijs. 1991. Shifting Boundaries: Trends in Religious and Educational Homogamy. *American Sociological Review.* 56(6): 786-800.

Kalmijn, Matthijs. 1996. The Socioeconomic Assimilation of Caribbean American Blacks. *Social Forces.* 74(3):911-930.

Kaufman, Robert. 2002. Assessing Alternative Perspectives on Race and Sex Employment. *American Sociological Review.* 67(4):547-572.

Keister, Lisa. 2000. *Wealth in America.* MA: Cambridge University Press.

Keister, Lisa and Stephanie Moller. 2000. Wealth Inequality in America. Annual Review of Sociology. Volume 26, pp. 63-81.

Kennedy, Randall. 1997. *Race, Crime, and the Law*. NY: Pantheon Books.

Kim, Kwang Chung and Won Moo Hurh. (1993). Beyond Assimilation and Pluralism; Syncretic Sociocultural and Adaptation of Korean Immigrants in the US. *Sociological Inquiry*. 64, 281-306.

Kreft, Ita and Jan de Leeuw. 2000. *Introducing Multilevel Modeling*. CA: Sage Publications.

Krysan, Maria and Reynolds Farley. 2002. The Residential Preferences of Blacks. *Social Forces*. Vol 80(3):937-980.

Krivo, Lauren and Robert Kaufman. 2004. Housing and Wealth Inequality: Racial-Ethnic Differences in Home Equity in the United States. Demography. 41:585-605.

Lang, Marvel. 1992. Barriers to Blacks' Educational Achievement in Higher Education: A Statistical and Conceptual Review. *Journal of Black Studies*, Vol. 22(4): 510-522.

Lee, Barrett, R.S. Oropesa and James Kanan. 1994. Neighborhood Context and Residential Mobility. *Demography* 31:249-270.

Levy, Frank. 1995. Incomes and Income Inequality. In *State of the Union*. Volume One. Edited by Reynolds Farley. 1-58.

Lewis, Amanda. 2002. Whiteness Studies: Past Research and Future Directions. *African American Research Perspectives*. 8(1):1-16.

Lewis Mumford Center. 2003. Black Diversity. www.albany.edu/mumford.

Lieberson, Stanley. 1980. *A Piece of the Pie*. CA: University of California Press.

Light, Ivan and Steven Gold. 2000. *Ethnic Economies*. CA: Academic Press.

Logan, John and Harvey Molotch. 1987. *Urban Forces*. CA: University of California Press.

Logan, John and Richard Alba. 1993. "Locational Returns to Human Capital: Minority Access to Suburban Community Resources" *Demography* 30(May): 243-268.

Logan, John R., Richard Alba and Shu-Yin Leung. 1996. Minority Access to White Suburbs: A Multiregional Comparison. *Social Forces*, Vol. 74(3):851-881.

Logan, John R, Richard Alba and Charles Zhang. 2002. Immigrant Enclaves and Ethnic Communities. *American Sociological Review*. 67(2): 299-322.

Long, Scott J. 1997. *Regression Models for Categorical and Limited Dependent Variables*. Thousand Oaks: Sage Publications.

Lowy, Michael. 1996. Figures of Weberian Marxism. *Theory and Society.@* 25(3): 431-446.

Mare, Robert. 1995. Changes in Educational Attainment and School Enrollment. In *State of the Union*. Volume One. Edited by Reynolds Farley. 1-58.

Massey, Douglas and Brendan Mullan. 1984. Processes of Hispanic and Black Spatial Assimilation. *American Journal of Sociology*. 89(4):836-873.

Massey, Douglas and Nancy Denton. 1993. *American Apartheid*. MA: Harvard University Press.

Massey, Douglas, Andrew Gross, and Kumiko Shibuya. 1994. Migration, Segregation and the Geographic Concentration of Poverty. *American Sociological Review* 59: 425-445.

McCall, Leslie. 2001. Sources of Racial Wage Inequality in Metropolitan Labor Markets. *American Sociological Review*. Vol 66(4): 520-541.

McDonald, John and Robert Moffitt. 1980. The Uses of Tobit Analysis. *The Review of Economics and Statistics*. 62(2): 318-21.

McLanahan, Sara and Lynne Casper. 1995. Growing Diversity and Inequality in the American Family, In *State of the Union. Volume Two*. Reynolds Farley, Editor. NY: Russell Sage Foundation.

Montagu, Ashley. 1997. *Man's Most Dangerous Myth: The Fallacy of Race.*

Morris, Aldon. 1984. *The Origins of the Civil Rights Movement.* NY: Free Press.

Moynihan, Daniel Patrick and Nathan Glazer. 1970. Beyond the Melting Pot. MA: MIT Press.

Mumford Center. 2003. *Black Diversity in Metropolitan America*. University at Albany. State University of New York.

Munford, Clarence. 1986. Slavery in the French Caribbean. *Journal of Black Studies*. 17(1): 49-69.

Myers, Dowell and Jennifer Wolch. 1995. The Polarization of Housing Status. In *State of the Union: America in the 1990s. Volume One: Economic Trends*, Edited by Reynolds Farley. New York: Russell Sage Foundation.

Omi, Michael and Howard Winant. 1994. *Racial Formation in the United States*. NY: Routledge.

Oliver, Melvin and Thomas Shapiro. 1995. *Black Wealth/White Wealth*. NY: Routledge.

Park, Robert. 1927. Human Nature and Collective Behavior. *American Journal of Sociology*, Vol. 32(5):733-741.

Park, Sun-Young. 1995. Childcare Expenditures of Households: Tobit Analyses for Different Family Types. *Family Economics and Resource Management Biennial.*

Pierce, Joseph. 1995. *Negro Business and Business Education*. Plenum Press.

Portes, Alejandro and Robert Bach. (1985). *Latin Journey.* Berkley: University of California Press.

Portes, Alejandro, Kyle, David and William Eaton. 1992. Mental Illness and Help-seeking Behavior among Mariel Cuban and Haitian Refugees in South Florida. *Journal of Health and Social Behavior*. 33(4): 283-298.

Portes, Alejandro and Ruben Rumbaut. (1996). *Immigrant America*. CA: University of California Press.

Portes, Alejandro, William Haller and Luis Eduardo Guarnizo. 2002. Transnational Entrepreneurs: An Alternative Form of Immigrant Economic Adaptation. *American Sociological Review*. 67:278-298.

Portes, Alejandro and Min Zhou. (1993). The New Second Generation. *The Annals*. (503): 74-96.

Rivera-Batiz, Francisco L. and Carlos E. Santiago. (1996). *Island Paradox*. New York : Russell Sage Foundation

Ross, Catherine, John Mirowsky and Shana Pribesh. 2001. Powerlessness and the Amplification of Threat: Neighborhood Disadvantage, Disorder, and Mistrust. *American Sociological Review*. 66(4):568-591.

Rushing, William and Suzanne Ortega. Socioeconomic Status and Mental Disorder: New Evidence and a Sociomedical Formulation. American Journal of Sociology. 84(5): 1175-1200.

Sander, William. 1993. Catholicism and Intermarriage in the United States. *Journal of Marriage and Family*. 55(4): 1037-1041.

Santiago, Anne and Margaret Wilder. (1991). Residential Segregation and Links to Minority Poverty: The Case of Latinos in the United States. *Social Problems*. (38):492-515.

St. Jean, Yanick and Joe Feagin. 1998. *Double Burden: Black Women and Everyday Racism*. NY: ME Sharpe.

Schoen, Robert and Robin M. Weinick. 1993. Partner Choice in Marriages and Cohabitations. *Journal of Marriage and Family*. 55(2):408-414.

Segal, Lewis and Daniel Sullivan. 1998. Trends in Homeowneship: Race, Demographics, and Income. Federal Reserve Bank of Chicago.

Shapiro, Thomas. 2001. The Importance of Assets. In *Assets for the Poor*. Thomas Shapiro and Edward Wolff, editors. NY: Russell Sage Foundation.

Shapiro, Thomas. 2005. The Hidden Cost of Being African-American: How Wealth Perpetuates Inequality. Oxford University Press.

Sherraden, Michael. 2001. Asset-Building Policy and Programs for the Poor. In *Assets for the Poor*. Shapiro, Thomas and Wolff, Edward, editors. 302-323. NY: Russell Sage Foundation.

Showers, Vince and Joyce Shotick. 1994. The Effects of Household Characteristics on Demand for Insurance: A Tobit Analysis. *Journal of Risk and Insurance*. 61(3): 492-502.

Skerry, Peter. 2000. Counting on the Census? *Race, Group Identity, and the Evasion of Politics.* Washington, D.C.: Brookings Institution Press.

Smedley, Audrey. 1999. *Race in North America*. Westview Press.

Smith, Cherly. 2000. If You Only Knew: Lessons Learned From Successful Black Women Entrepreneurs. *Journal for Pedagogy, Pluralism and Practice.*

Smith, A. Wade and Joan Moore. 1985. East-West Differences in Black Economic Development. *Journal of Black Studies*. 16(2):131-154.

South, Scott and Eric Baumer. 2000. Deciphering Community and Race Effects on Adolescent Premarital Childbearing. *Social Forces*. 78(4): 1379-1407.

South, Scott and Kyle D. Crowder. 1998. Leaving the Hood: Residential Mobility between Black, White, and Integrated Neighborhoods. *American Sociological Review* 63:17-26.

South, Scott and Kyle D. Crowder. 1999. Neighborhood Effects on Family Formation: Concentrated Poverty and Beyond. *American Sociological Review* 64:113-132.

South, Scott and Kyle Crowder. (2000). The Declining Significance of Neighborhoods? Marital Transitions in Community Context. *Social Forces* (78): 1067-1099.

Sowell, Thomas. 1981. *Markets and Minorities*. Oxford :Basil Blackwell for the International Center for Economic Policy Studies.

Spener, David and Frank Bean. 1999. Self-Employment Concentration and Earnings Among Mexican Immigrants in the U.S. Social Forces. 77(3): 1021-1047.

Stern, Mark. 2001. The Un(credit)worthy Poor. In *Assets for the Poor*. Shapiro, Thomas and Wolff, Edward, editors. 269-301. NY: Russell Sage Foundation.

Sykes, Lori. 2002. Wealth Inequalities Among and Between Asian, Black, Hispanic and White Women. *Journal of Intergroup Relations*. Volume 29: 3-15.

Sykes, Lori. 2005. A Home of Her Own. *Social Science Journal*.

Taylor, J. Edward. 2000. Do Government Programs Crowd In Remittances? Working Paper. University of California, Davis.

Tienda, Marta and Franklin Wilson. 1992. Migration and The Earnings of Hispanic Men. *American Sociological Review*. (57):661-678.

Tomaskovic-Devey, Donald. 2001. Race, Ethnic and Gender Earnings Inequality: The Sources and Consequences of Employment Segregation. *Glass Ceiling Commission, U. S. Department of Labor. Washington D.C.*

Tomich, Dale. 1986. World Slavery and Caribbean Capitalism. *Theory and Society*. 20(3): 297-319.

Tolnay, Stewart E. 1998. "Educational Selection in the Migration of Southern Blacks." *Social Forces* 77: 487-514.

Tolnay, Stewart E., and Beck, E.M. 1992. "Racial Violence and Black migration in the American South, 1910 to 1930." *American Sociological Review* 57: 103-114.

Tucker, Robert. 1978. *The Marx-Engels Reader.* Second Edition. New York: W.W. Norton & Company.

Ture, Kwame and Charles V. Hamilton. 1992. *Black Power: The Politics of Liberation.* NY: Vintage Books.

Turner, Margery Austin and Felicity Skidmore. 1999. *Mortgage Lending Discrimination: A Review of Existing Evidence.* The Urban Institute.

U.S. Census Bureau, Demographic Surveys Division, Continuous Measurement Office, August 22, 2002.

U.S. Census Bureau, Asset Ownership of Households: 1995.

U.S. Census Bureau, 1992 Economic Census. Minority-Owned Business Enterprises.

U.S. Census Bureau, 1997 Economic Census. Minority-Owned Business Enterprises.

U.S. Census Bureau, 1997 Economic Census. Women-Owned Businesses.

U.S. Department of Commerce. Economics and Statistics Administration. Statistical Briefs. Housing in Metropolitan Areas. 1995.

Waldinger, Roger and Mehdi Bozorgmehr. 1996. *Ethnic Los Angeles.* New York: Russell Sage Foundation.

Waters, Mary. 1994. Ethnic and Racial Identities of Second-Generation Black Immigrants in New York City. *International Migration Review.* 28(4):795-820.

West, Cornell. 2002. Toward a Socialist Theory of Racism. *Race and Ethnicity.* http://eserver.org/race/toward-a-theory-of-racism.html.

Willie, Charles Vert. 1981. *The Caste and Class Controversy on Race and Poverty*. Harvard University Press.

Willhelm, Mark. 2001. The Role of Intergenerational Transfers in Spreading Asset Ownership. In *Assets for the Poor.* Thomas Shapiro and Edward Wolff, editors. NY: Russell Sage Foundation.

Wilmoth, Janet. 2002. Does Marital History Matter?: The Effect of Marital Status on Wealth Outcomes Among Pre-Retirement Age Adults. Journal of Marriage and Family.

Wilson, Kenneth and Alejandro Portes. 1980. Immigrant Enclaves: An Analysis of the Labor Market Experiences of Cubans in Miami. American Journal of Sociology. 86(2): 295-319.

Wilson, William Julius. 1980. *The Declining Significance of Race*. Chicago University Press.

Wilson, William Julius. 1987. *The Truly Disadvantaged*. Chicago: Chicago University Press.

Wilson, William Julius. 1996. *When Work Disappears*. MA: Harvard University Press.

Wolff, Edward. 1995. "How the Pie is Sliced" *The American Prospect*. 22: 58-64 (http://epn.org/prospect/22/22wolf.html).

Yamashita, Takashi. 2002. Owner-Occupied Housing and Investment in Stocks: An Empirical Test. *Journal of Urban Economics*.

Yinger, John. 1999. Sustaining the Fair Housing Act. *Cityscape*. Volume 4, Number 3.

Zhou, Min. 1992. *Chinatown: The Socioeconomic Potential of an Urban Enclave*. PA: Temple University Press.

Zhou, Min and Carlton Bankston. (1995). Effects of Minority-Language Literacy on the Academic Achievement of Vietnamese Youth in New Orleans. *Sociology of Education*. (68): 1-17.

Zuberi, Tukufu. 2001. *Thicker than Blood.* Minneapolis: University of Minnesota Press.

ABOUT THE AUTHOR

Dr. Lori Latrice Sykes is Assistant Professor at John Jay College of Criminal Justice in the African-American Studies Department. She received her doctorate in sociology from the University of Albany, State University of New York. She is the author of a number of articles on race and wealth.